GREATEST SPEECHES OF VIVEKANANDA

GREATEST SPEECHES OF VIVEKANANDA

SWAMI VIVEKANANDA

Published by
PRABHAT PRAKASHAN PVT. LTD.
4/19 Asaf Ali Road,
New Delhi-110002 (INDIA)
e-mail: prabhatbooks@gmail.com

ISBN 978-93-5521-055-5
GREATEST SPEECHES OF VIVEKANANDA
by *Swami Vivekananda*

Edition
2025

Price
₹ 400 (Rupees Four Hundred Only)

Printed at
R-Tech Offset Printers, Delhi

Swami Vivekananda represented India and Hinduism at the Parliament of the World's Religions (1893). India Celebrates National youth day on birth anniversary of swami. This was the first World's Parliament of Religions, and it was held from 11 to 27 September 1893. Delegates from all over the world joined this Parliament. In 2012 a three-day world conference was organized to commemorate 150th birth anniversary of Vivekananda.

Publisher's Note

Very few people can leave an impression on the world through their speech, Swami Vivekananda was one such personality who changed millions of lives through his oration. His speech is a direct reflection of his thoughts, ideals, vision for the world and also his way of inspiring the youth. Though his speech is recorded and is made available even today, one must not forget that his speech is equally relevant today as it was years back. Vivekananda's speech shall eternally keep influencing the present generation as well as the generation ahead.

In the World's Parliament of Religions, Chicago, Vivekananda represented India and Hinduism in a rational manner and millions were awe struck after he had finished delivering his speech. He spoke on varied topics, right from the influence of Buddhism to the Ramayana and especially the role of women. It is believed that after his speech in Chicago, many became his disciple, they wanted to learn more from him and walk the path he had chosen. His speech has been and still is accounted as an example for many leaders around the world to inspire the people and teach them the significance of brotherhood. The values laid down by Swamiji is noteworthy in all aspect, especially for the younger generation of this world, who will lay the foundation of the future. Values like, compassion, tolerance, acceptance, is something we all should practice.

Swamiji dreamt for a better world and key to its betterment lies in his speeches. The valuable words and ideas he left behind for us is what the world requires the most and shall also need in the future. The relevance of his speech is equally meaningful even in the 21st century. His speech aims at not only building a nation without differences but also is essential to an individual's growth. It is like a torch that shall continue to bear light and show us the way amidst darkness of knowledge. It brings us together as world citizen and not divide us by borders and cultures. Vivekananda in speech spoke about unity, a unity that we can achieve by going beyond caste, creed, race, gender and class. It helps to reduce the gap between Nations and individuals and forms a bridge of brotherhood and acceptance across the planet. The speeches by Swamiji, entails ideas that if imbibed will help us to build a better world together – a world where we can live in harmony.

This book is a collection of his speeches at the conference and intends to inspire the readers with

Swamiji's words. It is the voice of Vivekananda that has been captured here, a voice that call us from our slumber of ignorance and leads us to the path of enlightenment and awakening. His speech can help us become a better version of ourselves. A core concept that he believed in was that of 'family' and how it can form the basis of harmony and brotherhood on a macro scale. His speeches does indicate towards accepting each other, like we do in a family. According to him, the whole world can form a family if they live with harmony and right tolerance. His speech also portrays the secularism of India, the country where he belonged and he was proud of the diversity and empathy. His speech should be read by everyone across the borders and one must understand the true depth of his words. The speeches in Chicago represent what Vivekananda truly believed in and what he stood for. His philosophies shall constantly inspire us and help move forward towards a bright and fruitful future.

❑

Table of Contents

Publisher's Note 7

1. Response to Welcome 13
2. Why We Disagree 16
3. Paper on Hinduism 19
4. Religion not the Crying Need of India 39
5. Buddhism, The Fulfilment of Hinduism 41
6. Address at the Final 45
7. The Spirit and Influence of Vedanta 48
8. The Soul and God 56
9. Practical Religion: Breathing and Meditation 76
10. The Gita I 88
11. The Gita II 105
12. Krishna 115

13. Mohammed 127

14. One Existence Appearing as Many 133

15. The Free Soul 147

16. Unity, The Goal of Religion 165

17. Bhakti 173

18. On Lord Buddha 186

19. The Ramayana 190

20. The Great Teachers of the World 211

21. Buddha's Message to the World 232

22. My Life and Mission 253

❑

Response to Welcome

At the World's Parliament of Religions, Chicago, 11th September, 1893

Sisters and Brothers of America

It fills my heart with joy unspeakable to rise in response to the warm and cordial welcome which you have given us. I thank you in the name of the most ancient order of monks in the world; I thank you in the name of the mother of religions; and I thank you in the name of millions and millions of Hindu people of all classes and sects.

My thanks, also, to some of the speakers on this platform who, referring to the delegates from the Orient, have told you that these men from far-off nations may well claim the honour of bearing to different lands the idea of toleration. I am proud to belong to a religion which has taught the world both tolerance and universal acceptance. We believe not only in universal toleration, but we accept all religions as true. I am proud to belong to a nation which has sheltered the persecuted and the refugees of all religions and all nations of the earth. I am proud to tell you that we have gathered in our bosom the purest remnant of the Israelites, who came to Southern India and took refuge with us in the very year in which their holy temple was shattered to pieces by Roman tyranny. I am proud to belong to the religion which has sheltered and is still fostering the remnant of the grand Zoroastrian nation. I will quote to you, brethren, a few lines from a hymn which I remember to have repeated from my earliest boyhood, which is every day repeated by millions of human beings: “As the different streams having their sources in different places all mingle their water in the sea, so, O Lord, the different paths which men take through different tendencies, various though they appear, crooked or straight, all lead to Thee.”

The present convention, which is one of the most august assemblies ever held, is in itself a vindication, a declaration to the world of the wonderful doctrine preached in the Gita: "Whosoever comes to Me, through whatsoever form, I reach him; all men are struggling through paths which in the end lead to me." Sectarianism, bigotry, and its horrible descendant, fanaticism, have long possessed this beautiful earth. They have filled the earth with violence, drenched it often and often with human blood, destroyed civilisation and sent whole nations to despair. Had it not been for these horrible demons, human society would be far more advanced than it is now. But their time is come; and I fervently hope that the bell that tolled this morning in honour of this convention may be the death-knell of all fanaticism, of all persecutions with the sword or with the pen, and of all uncharitable feelings between persons wending their way to the same goal.

❑

Why We Disagree

Delivered at the World's Parliament of Religions, Chicago, 15 September, 1893.

I will tell you a little story. You have heard the eloquent speaker who has just finished say, "Let us cease from abusing each other," and he was very sorry that there should be always so much variance.

But I think I should tell you a story which would illustrate the cause of this variance. A frog lived in a well. It had lived there for a long time. It was born there and brought up there, and yet was a little, small frog. Of course the evolutionists were not there then to tell us whether the frog lost its eyes or not, but, for our story's sake, we must take it for granted that it had its eyes, and that it every day cleansed the water of all the worms and bacilli that lived in it with an energy that would do credit to our modern bacteriologists. In this way it went on and became a little sleek and fat. Well, one day another frog that lived in the sea came and fell into the well.

"Where are you from?"

"I am from the sea."

"The sea! How big is that? Is it as big as my well?" and he took a leap from one side of the well to the other.

"My friend," said the frog of the sea, "how do you compare the sea with your little well?"

Then the frog took another leap and asked, "Is your sea so big?"

"What nonsense you speak, to compare the sea with your well!"

"Well, then," said the frog of the well, "nothing can be bigger than my well; there can be nothing bigger than this; this fellow is a liar, so turn him out."

That has been the difficulty all the while.

I am a Hindu. I am sitting in my own little well and thinking that the whole world is my little well. The Christian sits in his little well and thinks the whole world is his well. The Mohammedan sits in his little well and thinks that is the whole world. I have to thank you of America for the great attempt you are making to break down the barriers of this little world of ours, and hope that, in the future, the Lord will help you to accomplish your purpose.

❑

Paper on Hinduism

Read at the Parliament on 19th September, 1893

Three religions now stand in the world which have came down to us from time prehistoric – Hinduism, Zoroastrianism and Judaism. They have all received tremendous shocks and all of them prove by their survival their internal strength. But while Judaism failed to absorb Christianity and was driven out of its place of birth by its all-conquering daughter, and a handful of Parsees is all that remains to tell the tale of their grand religion, sect after sect arose in India and seemed to shake the religion of the Vedas to its very foundations, but like the waters of the seashore in a tremendous earthquake it receded only for a while, only to return in an all-absorbing flood, a thousand times more vigorous, and when the tumult of the rush was over, these sects were all sucked in, absorbed, and assimilated into the immense body of the mother faith.

From the high spiritual flights of the Vedanta philosophy, of which the latest discoveries of science seem like echoes, to the low ideas of idolatry with its multifarious mythology, the agnosticism of the Buddhists, and the atheism of the Jains, each and all have a place in the Hindu's religion.

Where then, the question arises, where is the common centre to which all these widely diverging radii converge? Where is the common basis upon which all these seemingly hopeless contradictions rest? And this is the question I shall attempt to answer.

The Hindus have received their religion through revelation, the Vedas. They hold that the Vedas are without beginning and without end. It may sound ludicrous to this audience, how a book can be without beginning or end. But by the Vedas no books are meant. They mean the accumulated treasury of spiritual laws discovered by different persons in different times. Just as the law of gravitation existed before its discovery, and would exist if all humanity forgot it, so is it with the laws that govern the spiritual world. The moral, ethical, and spiritual relations between soul and soul and between individual spirits and the Father of all spirits, were there before their discovery, and would remain even if we forgot them.

The discoverers of these laws are called Rishis, and we honour them as perfected beings. I am glad to tell this audience that some of the very greatest of them were women. Here it may be said that these laws as laws may be without end, but they must have had a beginning. The Vedas teach us that creation is without beginning or end. Science is said to have proved that the sum total of cosmic energy is always the same. Then, if there was a time when nothing existed, where was all this manifested energy? Some say it was in a potential form in God. In that case God is sometimes potential and sometimes kinetic, which would make Him mutable. Everything mutable is a compound, and everything compound must undergo that change which is called destruction. So God would die, which is absurd. Therefore there never was a time when there was no creation.

If I may be allowed to use a simile, creation and creator are two lines, without beginning and without end, running parallel to each other. God is the ever active providence, by whose power systems after systems are being evolved out of chaos, made to run for a time and again destroyed. This is what the Brâhmin boy repeats every day: "The sun and the moon, the Lord created like the suns and moons of previous cycles." And this agrees with modern science.

Here I stand and if I shut my eyes, and try to conceive my existence, "I", "I", "I", what is the idea before me? The idea of a body. Am I, then, nothing but a combination of material substances? The Vedas declare, "No". I am a spirit living in a body. I am not the body. The body will die, but I shall not die. Here am I in this body; it will fall, but I shall go on living. I had also a past. The soul was not created, for creation means a combination which means a certain future dissolution. If then the soul was created, it must die. Some are born happy, enjoy perfect health, with beautiful body, mental vigour and all wants supplied. Others are born miserable, some are without hands or feet, others again are idiots and only drag on a wretched existence. Why, if they are all created, why does a just and merciful God create one happy and another unhappy, why is He so partial? Nor would it mend matters in the least to hold that those who are miserable in this life will be happy in a future one. Why should a man be miserable even here in the reign of a just and merciful God?

In the second place, the idea of a creator God does not explain the anomaly, but simply expresses the cruel fiat of an all-powerful being. There must have been causes, then, before his birth, to make a man miserable or happy and those were his past actions.

Are not all the tendencies of the mind and the body accounted for by inherited aptitude? Here are two parallel lines of existence – one of the mind, the other of matter. If matter and its transformations answer for all that we have, there is no necessity for supposing the existence of a soul. But it cannot be proved that thought has been evolved out of matter, and if a philosophical monism is inevitable, spiritual monism is certainly logical and no less desirable than a materialistic monism; but neither of these is necessary here.

We cannot deny that bodies acquire certain tendencies from heredity, but those tendencies only mean the physical configuration, through which a peculiar mind alone can act in a peculiar way. There are other tendencies peculiar to a soul caused by its past actions. And a soul with a certain tendency would by the laws of affinity take birth in a body which is the fittest instrument for the display of that tendency. This is in accord with science, for science wants to explain everything by habit, and habit is got through repetitions. So repetitions are necessary to explain the natural habits of a new-born soul. And since they were not obtained in this present life, they must have come down from past lives.

There is another suggestion. Taking all these for granted, how is it that I do not remember anything of my past life ? This can be easily explained. I am now speaking English. It is not my mother tongue, in fact no words of my mother tongue are now present in my consciousness; but let me try to bring them up, and they rush in. That shows that consciousness is only the surface of the mental ocean, and within its depths are stored up all our experiences. Try and struggle, they would come up and you would be conscious even of your past life.

This is direct and demonstrative evidence. Verification is the perfect proof of a theory, and here is the challenge thrown to the world by the Rishis. We have discovered the secret by which the very depths of the ocean of memory can be stirred up – try it and you would get a complete reminiscence of your past life.

So then the Hindu believes that he is a spirit. Him the sword cannot pierce – him the fire cannot burn – him the water cannot melt – him the air cannot dry. The Hindu believes that every soul is a circle whose circumference is nowhere, but whose centre is located in the body, and that death means the change of this centre from body to body. Nor is the soul bound by the conditions of matter. In its very essence it is free, unbounded, holy, pure, and perfect. But somehow or other it finds itself tied down to matter, and thinks of itself as matter.

Why should the free, perfect, and pure being be thus under the thraldom of matter, is the next question. How can the perfect soul be deluded into the belief that it is imperfect? We have been told that the Hindus shirk the question and say that no such question can be there. Some thinkers want to answer it by positing one or more quasi-perfect beings, and use big scientific names to fill up the gap. But naming is not explaining. The question remains the same. How can the perfect become the quasi-perfect; how can the pure, the absolute, change even a microscopic particle of its nature? But the Hindu is sincere. He does not want to take shelter under sophistry. He is brave enough to face the question in a manly fashion; and his answer is: "I do not know. I do not know how the perfect being, the soul, came to think of itself as imperfect, as joined to and conditioned by matter." But the fact is a fact for all that. It is a fact in everybody's consciousness that one thinks of oneself as the body. The Hindu does not attempt to explain why one thinks one is the body. The answer that it is the will of God is no explanation. This is nothing more than what the Hindu says, "I do not know."

Well, then, the human soul is eternal and immortal, perfect and infinite, and death means only a change of centre from one body to another. The present is determined by our past actions, and the future by the present. The soul will go on evolving up or reverting back from birth to birth and death to death. But here is another question: Is man a tiny boat in a tempest, raised one moment on the foamy crest of a billow and dashed down into a yawning chasm the next, rolling to and fro at the mercy of good and bad actions – a powerless, helpless wreck in an ever-raging, ever-rushing, uncompromising current of cause and effect; a little moth placed under the wheel of causation which rolls on crushing everything in its way and waits not for the widow's tears or the orphan's cry? The heart sinks at the idea, yet this is the law of Nature. Is there no hope? Is there no escape? – was the cry that went up from the bottom of the heart of despair. It reached the throne of mercy, and words of hope and consolation came down and inspired a Vedic sage, and he stood up before the world and in trumpet voice proclaimed the glad tidings: "Hear, ye children of immortal bliss! even ye that reside in higher spheres! I have found the Ancient One who is beyond all darkness, all delusion: knowing Him alone you shall be saved from death over again." "Children of immortal bliss" – what a sweet, what a hopeful name! Allow me to call you, brethren, by that sweet name – heirs of immortal bliss – yea, the Hindu refuses to call you sinners. Ye are the Children of God, the sharers of immortal bliss, holy and perfect beings. Ye divinities on earth – sinners! It is a sin to call a man so; it is a standing libel on human nature. Come up, O lions, and shake off the delusion that you are sheep; you are souls immortal, spirits free, blest and eternal;

ye are not matter, ye are not bodies; matter is your servant, not you the servant of matter.

Thus it is that the Vedas proclaim not a dreadful combination of unforgiving laws, not an endless prison of cause and effect, but that at the head of all these laws, in and through every particle of matter and force, stands One "by whose command the wind blows, the fire burns, the clouds rain, and death stalks upon the earth."

And what is His nature?

He is everywhere, the pure and formless One, the Almighty and the All-merciful. "Thou art our father, Thou art our mother, Thou art our beloved friend, Thou art the source of all strength; give us strength. Thou art He that beareth the burdens of the universe; help me bear the little burden of this life." Thus sang the Rishis of the Vedas. And how to worship Him? Through love. "He is to be worshipped as the one beloved, dearer than everything in this and the next life."

This is the doctrine of love declared in the Vedas, and let us see how it is fully developed and taught by Krishna, whom the Hindus believe to have been God incarnate on earth.

He taught that a man ought to live in this world like a lotus leaf, which grows in water but is never moistened by water; so a man ought to live in the world – his heart to God and his hands to work.

It is good to love God for hope of reward in this or the next world, but it is better to love God for love's sake, and the prayer goes: "Lord, I do not want wealth, nor children, nor learning. If it be Thy will, I shall go from birth to birth, but grant me this, that I may love Thee without the hope of reward – love unselfishly for love's sake." One of the disciples of Krishna, the then Emperor of India, was driven from his kingdom by his enemies and had to take shelter with his queen in a forest in the Himalayas, and there one day the queen asked him how it was that he, the most virtuous of men, should suffer so much misery. Yudhishthira answered, "Behold, my queen, the Himalayas, how grand and beautiful they are; I love them. They do not give me anything, but my nature is to love the grand, the beautiful, therefore I love them. Similarly, I love the Lord. He is the source of all beauty, of all sublimity. He is the only object to be loved; my nature is to love Him, and therefore I love. I do not pray for anything; I do not ask for anything. Let Him place me wherever He likes. I must love Him for love's sake. I cannot trade in love."

The Vedas teach that the soul is divine, only held in the bondage of matter; perfection will be reached when this bond will burst, and the word they use for it is therefore, Mukti – freedom, freedom from the bonds of imperfection, freedom from death and misery.

And this bondage can only fall off through the mercy of God, and this mercy comes on the pure. So purity is the condition of His mercy. How does that mercy act? He reveals Himself to the pure heart; the pure and the stainless see God, yea, even in this life; then and then only all the crookedness of the heart is made straight. Then all doubt ceases. He is no more the freak of a terrible law of causation. This is the very centre, the very vital conception of Hinduism. The Hindu does not want to live upon words and theories. If there are existences beyond the ordinary sensuous existence, he wants to come face to face with them. If there is a soul in him which is not matter, if there is an all-merciful universal Soul, he will go to Him direct. He must see Him, and that alone can destroy all doubts. So the best proof a Hindu sage gives about the soul, about God, is: "I have seen the soul; I have seen God." And that is the only condition of perfection. The Hindu religion does not consist in struggles and attempts to believe a certain doctrine or dogma, but in realising – not in believing, but in being and becoming.

Thus the whole object of their system is by constant struggle to become perfect, to become divine, to reach God and see God, and this reaching God, seeing God, becoming perfect even as the Father in Heaven is perfect, constitutes the religion of the Hindus.

And what becomes of a man when he attains perfection? He lives a life of bliss infinite. He enjoys infinite and perfect bliss, having obtained the only thing in which man ought to have pleasure, namely God, and enjoys the bliss with God.

So far all the Hindus are agreed. This is the common religion of all the sects of India; but, then, perfection is absolute, and the absolute cannot be two or three. It cannot have any qualities. It cannot be an individual. And so when a soul becomes perfect and absolute, it must become one with Brahman, and it would only realise the Lord as the perfection, the reality, of its own nature and existence, the existence absolute, knowledge absolute, and bliss absolute. We have often and often read this called the losing of individuality and becoming a stock or a stone.

"He jests at scars that never felt a wound."

I tell you it is nothing of the kind. If it is happiness to enjoy the consciousness of this small body, it must be greater happiness to enjoy the consciousness of two bodies, the measure of happiness increasing with the consciousness of an increasing number of bodies, the aim, the ultimate of happiness being reached when it would become a universal consciousness.

Therefore, to gain this infinite universal individuality, this miserable little prison-individuality must go. Then alone can death cease when I am alone with life, then alone can misery cease when I am one with happiness itself, then alone can all errors cease when I am one with knowledge itself; and this is the necessary scientific conclusion. Science has proved to me that physical individuality is a delusion, that really my body is one little continuously changing body in an unbroken ocean of matter; and Advaita (unity) is the necessary conclusion with my other counterpart, soul.

Science is nothing but the finding of unity. As soon as science would reach perfect unity, it would stop from further progress, because it would reach the goal. Thus Chemistry could not progress farther when it would discover one element out of which all other could be made. Physics would stop when it would be able to fulfill its services in discovering one energy of which all others are but manifestations, and the science of religion become perfect when it would discover Him who is the one life in a universe of death, Him who is the constant basis of an ever-changing world. One who is the only Soul of which all souls are but delusive manifestations. Thus is it, through multiplicity and duality, that the ultimate unity is reached. Religion can go no farther. This is the goal of all science.

All science is bound to come to this conclusion in the long run. Manifestation, and not creation, is the word of science today, and the Hindu is only glad that what he has been cherishing in his bosom for ages is going to be taught in more forcible language, and with further light from the latest conclusions of science.

Descend we now from the aspirations of philosophy to the religion of the ignorant. At the very outset, I may tell you that there is no polytheism in India. In every temple, if one stands by and listens, one will find the worshippers applying all the attributes of God, including omnipresence, to the images. It is not polytheism, nor would the name henotheism explain the situation. "The rose called by any other name would smell as sweet." Names are not explanations.

I remember, as a boy, hearing a Christian missionary preach to a crowd in India. Among other sweet things he was telling them was that if he gave a blow to their idol with his stick, what could it do? One of his hearers sharply answered, "If I abuse your God, what can He do?" "You would be punished," said the preacher, "when you die." "So my idol will punish you when you die," retorted the Hindu.

The tree is known by its fruits. When I have seen amongst them that are called idolaters, men, the like of whom in morality and spirituality and love I have never seen anywhere, I stop and ask myself, "Can sin beget holiness?"

Superstition is a great enemy of man, but bigotry is worse. Why does a Christian go to church? Why is the cross holy? Why is the face turned toward the sky in prayer? Why are there so many images in the Catholic Church? Why are there so many images in the minds of Protestants when they pray? My brethren, we can no more think about anything without a mental image than we can live without breathing. By the law of association, the material image calls up the mental idea and vice versa. This is why the Hindu uses an external symbol when he worships. He will tell you, it helps to keep his mind fixed on the Being to whom he prays. He knows as well as you do that the image is not God, is not omnipresent. After all, how much does omnipresence mean to almost the whole world? It stands merely as a word, a symbol. Has God superficial area? If not, when we repeat that word "omnipresent", we think of the extended sky or of space, that is all.

As we find that somehow or other, by the laws of our mental constitution, we have to associate our ideas of infinity with the image of the blue sky, or of the sea, so we naturally connect our idea of holiness with the image of a church, a mosque, or a cross. The Hindus have associated the idea of holiness, purity, truth, omnipresence, and such other ideas with different images and forms. But with this difference that while some people devote their whole lives to their idol of a church and never rise higher, because with them religion means an intellectual assent to certain doctrines and doing good to their fellows, the whole religion of the Hindu is centred in realisation. Man is to become divine by realising the divine. Idols or temples or churches or books are only the supports, the helps, of his spiritual childhood: but on and on he must progress.

He must not stop anywhere. "External worship, material worship," say the scriptures, "is the lowest stage; struggling to rise high, mental prayer is the next stage, but the highest stage is when the Lord has been realised." Mark, the same earnest man who is kneeling before the idol tells you, "Him the Sun cannot express, nor the moon, nor the stars, the lightning cannot express Him, nor what we speak of as fire; through Him they shine." But he does not abuse any one's idol or call its worship sin. He recognises in it a necessary stage of life. "The child is father of the man." Would it be right for an old man to say that childhood is a sin or youth a sin?

If a man can realise his divine nature with the help of an image, would it be right to call that a sin? Nor even when he has passed that stage, should he call it an error. To the Hindu, man is not travelling from error to truth, but from truth to truth, from lower to higher truth. To him all the religions, from the lowest fetishism to the highest absolutism, mean so many attempts of the human soul to grasp and realise the Infinite, each determined by the conditions of its birth and association, and each of these marks a stage of progress; and every soul is a young eagle soaring higher and higher, gathering more and more strength, till it reaches the Glorious Sun.

Unity in variety is the plan of nature, and the Hindu has recognised it. Every other religion lays down certain fixed dogmas, and tries to force society to adopt them. It places before society only one coat which must fit Jack and John and Henry, all alike. If it does not fit John or Henry, he must go without a coat to cover his body. The Hindus have discovered that the absolute can only be realised, or thought of, or stated, through the relative, and the images, crosses, and crescents are simply so many symbols – so many pegs to hang the spiritual ideas on. It is not that this help is necessary for every one, but those that do not need it have no right to say that it is wrong. Nor is it compulsory in Hinduism.

One thing I must tell you. Idolatry in India does not mean anything horrible. It is not the mother of harlots. On the other hand, it is the attempt of undeveloped minds to grasp high spiritual truths. The Hindus have their faults, they sometimes have their exceptions; but mark this, they are always for punishing their own bodies, and never for cutting the throats of their neighbours. If the Hindu fanatic burns himself on the pyre, he never lights the fire of Inquisition. And even this cannot be laid at the door of his religion any more than the burning of witches can be laid at the door of Christianity.

To the Hindu, then, the whole world of religions is only a travelling, a coming up, of different men and women, through various conditions and circumstances, to the same goal. Every religion is only evolving a God out of the material man, and the same God is the inspirer of all of them. Why, then, are there so many contradictions? They are only apparent, says the Hindu. The contradictions come from the same truth adapting itself to the varying circumstances of different natures.

It is the same light coming through glasses of different colours. And these little variations are necessary for purposes of adaptation. But in the heart of everything the same truth reigns. The Lord has declared to the Hindu in His incarnation as Krishna, "I am in every religion as the thread through a string of pearls. Wherever thou seest extraordinary holiness and extraordinary power raising and purifying humanity, know thou that I am there." And what has been the result? I challenge the world to find, throughout the whole system of Sanskrit philosophy, any such expression as that the Hindu alone will be saved and not others. Says Vyasa, "We find perfect men even beyond the pale of our caste and creed." One thing more. How, then, can the Hindu, whose whole fabric of thought centres in God, believe in Buddhism which is agnostic, or in Jainism which is atheistic?

The Buddhists or the Jains do not depend upon God; but the whole force of their religion is directed to the great central truth in every religion, to evolve a God out of man. They have not seen the Father, but they have seen the Son. And he that hath seen the Son hath seen the Father also.

This, brethren, is a short sketch of the religious ideas of the Hindus. The Hindu may have failed to carry out all his plans, but if there is ever to be a universal religion, it must be one which will have no location in place or time; which will be infinite like the God it will preach, and whose sun will shine upon the followers of Krishna and of Christ, on saints and sinners alike; which will not be Brahminic or Buddhistic, Christian or Mohammedan, but the sum total of all these, and still have infinite space for development; which in its catholicity will embrace in its infinite arms, and find a place for, every human being, from the lowest grovelling savage not far removed from the brute, to the highest man towering by the virtues of his head and heart almost above humanity, making society stand in awe of him and doubt his human nature. It will be a religion which will have no place for persecution or intolerance in its polity, which will recognise divinity in every man and woman, and whose whole scope, whose whole force, will be created in aiding humanity to realise its own true, divine nature.

Offer such a religion, and all the nations will follow you. Asoka's council was a council of the Buddhist faith. Akbar's, though more to the purpose, was only a parlour-meeting. It was reserved for America to proclaim to all quarters of the globe that the Lord is in every religion.

May He who is the Brahman of the Hindus, the Ahura-Mazda of the Zoroastrians, the Buddha of the Buddhists, the Jehovah of the Jews, the Father in Heaven of the Christians, give strength to you to carry out your noble idea! The star arose in the East; it travelled steadily towards the West, sometimes dimmed and sometimes effulgent, till it made a circuit of the world; and now it is again rising on the very horizon of the East, the borders of the Sanpo , a thousandfold more effulgent than it ever was before.

Hail, Columbia, motherland of liberty! It has been given to thee, who never dipped her hand in her neighbour's blood, who never found out that the shortest way of becoming rich was by robbing one's neighbours, it has been given to thee to march at the vanguard of civilisation with the flag of harmony.

❑

Religion not the Crying Need of India

Delivered on 20th September, 1893

Christians must always be ready for good criticism, and I hardly think that you will mind if I make a little criticism. You Christians, who are so fond of sending out missionaries to save the soul of the heathen – why do you not try to save their bodies from starvation? In India, during the terrible famines, thousands died from hunger, yet you Christians did nothing. You erect churches all through India, but the crying evil in the East is not religion – they have religion enough – but it is bread that the suffering millions of burning India cry out for with parched throats. They ask us for bread, but we give them stones. It is an insult to a starving people to offer them religion; it is an insult to a starving man to teach him metaphysics. In India a priest that preached for money would lose caste and be spat upon by the people. I came here to seek aid for my impoverished people, and I fully realised how difficult it was to get help for heathens from Christians in a Christian land.

❑

Buddhism,
The Fulfilment of Hinduism

Delivered on 26th September, 1893

I am not a Buddhist, as you have heard, and yet I am. If China, or Japan, or Srilanka follow the teachings of the Great Master, India worships him as God incarnate on earth. You have just now heard that I am going to criticise Buddhism, but by that I wish you to understand only this. Far be it from me to criticise him whom I worship as God incarnate on earth. But our views about Buddha are that he was not understood properly by his disciples. The relation between Hinduism (by Hinduism, I mean the religion of the Vedas) and what is called Buddhism at the present day is nearly the same as between Judaism and Christianity. Jesus Christ was a Jew, and Shâkya Muni was a Hindu. The Jews rejected Jesus Christ, nay, crucified him, and the Hindus have accepted Shâkya Muni as God and worship him. But the real difference that we Hindus want to show between modern Buddhism and what we should understand as the teachings of Lord Buddha lies principally in this: Shâkya Muni came to preach nothing new. He also, like Jesus, came to fulfil and not to destroy. Only, in the case of Jesus, it was the old people, the Jews, who did not understand him, while in the case of Buddha, it was his own followers who did not realise the import of his teachings. As the Jew did not understand the fulfilment of the Old Testament, so the Buddhist did not understand the fulfilment of the truths of the Hindu religion. Again, I repeat, Shâkya Muni came not to destroy, but he was the fulfilment, the logical conclusion, the logical development of the religion of the Hindus.

The religion of the Hindus is divided into two parts: the ceremonial and the spiritual. The spiritual portion is specially studied by the monks.

In that there is no caste. A man from the highest caste and a man from the lowest may become a monk in India, and the two castes become equal. In religion there is no caste; caste is simply a social institution. Shâkya Muni himself was a monk, and it was his glory that he had the large-heartedness to bring out the truths from the hidden Vedas and through them broadcast all over the world. He was the first being in the world who brought missionarising into practice – nay, he was the first to conceive the idea of proselytising.

The great glory of the Master lay in his wonderful sympathy for everybody, especially for the ignorant and the poor. Some of his disciples were Brahmins. When Buddha was teaching, Sanskrit was no more the spoken language in India. It was then only in the books of the learned. Some of Buddha's Brahmins disciples wanted to translate his teachings into Sanskrit, but he distinctly told them, "I am for the poor, for the people; let me speak in the tongue of the people." And so to this day the great bulk of his teachings are in the vernacular of that day in India.

Whatever may be the position of philosophy, whatever may be the position of metaphysics, so long as there is such a thing as death in the world, so long as there is such a thing as weakness in the human heart, so long as there is a cry going out of the heart of man in his very weakness, there shall be a faith in God.

On the philosophic side the disciples of the Great Master dashed themselves against the eternal rocks of the Vedas and could not crush them, and on the other side they took away from the nation that eternal God to which every one, man or woman, clings so fondly. And the result was that Buddhism had to die a natural death in India. At the present day there is not one who calls oneself a Buddhist in India, the land of its birth.

But at the same time, Brahminism lost something – that reforming zeal, that wonderful sympathy and charity for everybody, that wonderful heaven which Buddhism had brought to the masses and which had rendered Indian society so great that a Greek historian who wrote about India of that time was led to say that no Hindu was known to tell an untruth and no Hindu woman was known to be unchaste.

Hinduism cannot live without Buddhism, nor Buddhism without Hinduism. Then realise what the separation has shown to us, that the Buddhists cannot stand without the brain and philosophy of the Brahmins, nor the Brahmin without the heart of the Buddhist. This separation between the Buddhists and the Brahmins is the cause of the downfall of India. That is why India is populated by three hundred millions of beggars, and that is why India has been the slave of conquerors for the last thousand years. Let us then join the wonderful intellect of the Brahmins with the heart, the noble soul, the wonderful humanising power of the Great Master.

❑

Address at the Final

Delivered on 27th September, 1893

The World's Parliament of Religions has become an accomplished fact, and the merciful Father has helped those who laboured to bring it into existence, and crowned with success their most unselfish labour.

My thanks to those noble souls whose large hearts and love of truth first dreamed this wonderful dream and then realised it. My thanks to the shower of liberal sentiments that has overflowed this platform. My thanks to his enlightened audience for their uniform kindness to me and for their appreciation of every thought that tends to smooth the friction of religions. A few jarring notes were heard from time to time in this harmony. My special thanks to them, for they have, by their striking contrast, made general harmony the sweeter.

Much has been said of the common ground of religious unity. I am not going just now to venture my own theory. But if any one here hopes that this unity will come by the triumph of any one of the religions and the destruction of the others, to him I say, "Brother, yours is an impossible hope." Do I wish that the Christian would become Hindu? God forbid. Do I wish that the Hindu or Buddhist would become Christian? God forbid.

The seed is put in the ground, and earth and air and water are placed around it. Does the seed become the earth; or the air, or the water? No. It becomes a plant, it develops after the law of its own growth, assimilates the air, the earth, and the water, converts them into plant substance, and grows into a plant.

Similar is the case with religion. The Christian is not to become a Hindu or a Buddhist, nor a Hindu or a Buddhist to become a Christian. But each must assimilate the spirit of the others and yet preserve his individuality and grow according to his own law of growth.

If the Parliament of Religions has shown anything to the world it is this: It has proved to the world that holiness, purity and charity are not the exclusive possessions of any church in the world, and that every system has produced men and women of the most exalted character. In the face of this evidence, if anybody dreams of the exclusive survival of his own religion and the destruction of the others, I pity him from the bottom of my heart, and point out to him that upon the banner of every religion will soon be written, in spite of resistance: “Help and not Fight,” “Assimilation and not Destruction,” “Harmony and Peace and not Dissension.”

❑

The Spirit and Influence of Vedanta

Delivered at the Twentieth Century Club, Boston

Before going into the subject of this afternoon, will you allow me to say a few words of thanks, now that I have the opportunity? I have lived three years amongst you. I have travelled over nearly the whole of America, and as I am going back from here to my own country, it is meet that I should take this opportunity of expressing my gratitude in this Athens of America. When I first came to this country, after a few days I thought I would be able to write a book on the nation. But after three years' stay here, I find I am not able to write even a page. On the other hand, I find in travelling in various countries that beneath the surface differences that we find in dress and food and little details of manners, man is man all the world over; the same wonderful human nature is everywhere represented. Yet there are certain characteristics, and in a few words I would like to sum up all my experiences here. In this land of America, no question is asked about a man's peculiarities. If a man is a man, that is enough, and they take him into their hearts, and that is one thing I have never seen in any other country in the world.

I came here to represent a philosophy of India, which is called the Vedanta philosophy. This philosophy is very, very ancient; it is the outcome of that mass of ancient Aryan literature known by the name of the Vedas. It is, as it were, the very flower of all the speculations and experiences and analyses, embodied in that mass of literature – collected and culled through centuries. This Vedanta philosophy has certain peculiarities. In the first place, it is perfectly impersonal; it does not owe its origin to any person or prophet: it does not build itself around one man as a centre. Yet it has nothing to say against philosophies which do build themselves around certain persons. In later days in India, other philosophies and systems arose, built around certain persons – such as Buddhism, or many of our present sects. They each have a certain leader to whom they owe allegiance, just as the Christians and Mohammedans have. But the Vedanta philosophy stands at the background of all these various sects, and there is no fight and no antagonism between the Vedanta and any other system in the world.

One principle it lays down – and that, the Vedanta claims, is to be found in every religion in the world – that man is divine, that all this which we see around us is the outcome of that consciousness of the divine. Everything that is strong, and good, and powerful in human nature is the outcome of that divinity, and though potential in many, there is no difference between man and man essentially, all being alike divine. There is, as it were, an infinite ocean behind, and you and I are so many waves, coming out of that infinite ocean; and each one of us is trying his best to manifest that infinite outside. So, potentially, each one of us has that infinite ocean of Existence, Knowledge, and Bliss as our birthright, our real nature; and the difference between us is caused by the greater or lesser power to manifest that divine. Therefore the Vedanta lays down that each man should be treated not as what he manifests, but as what he stands for. Each human being stands for the divine, and, therefore, every teacher should be helpful, not by condemning man, but by helping him to call forth the divinity that is within him.

It also teaches that all the vast mass of energy that we see displayed in society and in every plane of action is really from inside out; and, therefore, what is called inspiration by other sects, the Vedantist begs the liberty to call the expiration of man. At the same time it does not quarrel with other sects; the Vedanta has no quarrel with those who do not understand this divinity of man. Consciously or unconsciously, every man is trying to unfold that divinity.

Man is like an infinite spring, coiled up in a small box, and that spring is trying to unfold itself; and all the social phenomena that we see the result of this trying to unfold. All the competitions and struggles and evils that we see around us are neither the causes of these unfoldments, nor the effects. As one of our great philosophers says – in the case of the irrigation of a field, the tank is somewhere upon a higher level, and the water is trying to rush into the field, and is barred by a gate. But as soon as the gate is opened, the water rushes in by its own nature; and if there is dust and dirt in the way, the water rolls over them. But dust and dirt are neither the result nor the cause of this unfolding of the divine nature of man. They are coexistent circumstances, and, therefore, can be remedied.

Now, this idea, claims the Vedanta, is to be found in all religions, whether in India or outside of it;

only, in some of them, the idea is expressed through mythology, and in others, through symbology. The Vedanta claims that there has not been one religious inspiration, one manifestation of the divine man, however great, but it has been the expression of that infinite oneness in human nature; and all that we call ethics and morality and doing good to others is also but the manifestation of this oneness. There are moments when every man feels that he is one with the universe, and he rushes forth to express it, whether he knows it or not. This expression of oneness is what we call love and sympathy, and it is the basis of all our ethics and morality. This is summed up in the Vedanta philosophy by the celebrated aphorism, Tat Tvam Asi, "Thou art That".

To every man, this is taught: Thou art one with this Universal Being, and, as such, every soul that exists is your soul; and every body that exists is your body; and in hurting anyone, you hurt yourself, in loving anyone, you love yourself. As soon as a current of hatred is thrown outside, whomsoever else it hurts, it also hurts yourself; and if love comes out from you, it is bound to come back to you. For I am the universe; this universe is my body. I am the Infinite, only I am not conscious of it now; but I am struggling to get this consciousness of the Infinite, and perfection will be reached when full consciousness of this Infinite comes.

Another peculiar idea of the Vedanta is that we must allow this infinite variation in religious thought, and not try to bring everybody to the same opinion, because the goal is the same. As the Vedantist says in his poetical language, "As so many rivers, having their source in different mountains, roll down, crooked or straight, and at last come into the ocean – so, all these various creeds and religions, taking their start from different standpoints and running through crooked or straight courses, at last come unto THEE."

As a manifestation of that, we find that this most ancient philosophy has, through its influence, directly inspired Buddhism, the first missionary religion of the world, and indirectly, it has also influenced Christianity, through the Alexandrians, the Gnostics, and the European philosophers of the middle ages. And later, influencing German thought, it has produced almost a revolution in the regions of philosophy and psychology. Yet all this mass of influence has been given to the world almost unperceived. As the gentle falling of the dew at night brings support to all vegetable life, so, slowly and imperceptibly, this divine philosophy has been spread through the world for the good of mankind. No march of armies has been used to preach this religion. In Buddhism, one of the most missionary religions of the world, we find inscriptions remaining of the great Emperor Asoka – recording how missionaries were sent to Alexandria, to Antioch, to Persia, to China, and to various other countries of the then civilised world. Three hundred years before Christ, instructions were given them not to revile other religions: "The basis of all religions is the same, wherever they are; try to help them all you can, teach them all you can, but do not try to injure them."

Thus in India there never was any religious persecution by the Hindus, but only that wonderful reverence, which they have for all the religions of the world. They sheltered a portion of the Hebrews, when they were driven out of their own country; and the Malabar Jews remain as a result. They received at another time the remnant of the Persians, when they were almost annihilated; and they remain to this day, as a part of us and loved by us, as the modern Parsees of Bombay. There were Christians who claimed to have come with St. Thomas, the disciple of Jesus Christ; and they were allowed to settle in India and hold their own opinions; and a colony of them is even now in existence in India. And this spirit of toleration has not died out. It will not and cannot die there.

This is one of the great lessons that the Vedanta has to teach. Knowing that, consciously or unconsciously, we are struggling to reach the same goal, why should we be impatient? If one man is slower than another, we need not be impatient, we need not curse him, or revile him. When our eyes are opened and the heart is purified, the work of the same divine influence, the unfolding of the same divinity in every human heart, will become manifest; and then alone we shall be in a position to claim the brotherhood of man.

When a man has reached the highest, when he sees neither man nor woman, neither sect nor creed, nor colour, nor birth, nor any of these differentiations, but goes beyond and finds that divinity which is the real man behind every human being – then alone he has reached the universal brotherhood, and that man alone is a Vedantist.

Such are some of the practical historical results of the Vedanta.

❑

The Soul and God

This article was recorded by Ida Ansell in shorthand. As, however, Swamiji's speed was too great for her in her early days, dots are put in the articles to indicate the omissions, while the words within square brackets are added by way of linking up the disconnected parts.

Delivered in San Francisco, March 23, 1900

Whether it was fear or mere inquisitiveness which first led man to think of powers superior to himself, we need not discuss. These raised in the mind peculiar worship tendencies, and so on. There never have been [times in the history of mankind] without [some ideal] of worship. Why? What makes us all struggle for something beyond what we see – whether it be a beautiful morning or a fear of dead spirits? ... We need not go back into prehistoric times, for it is a fact present today as it was two thousand years ago. We do not find satisfaction here. Whatever our station in life – [even if we are] powerful and wealthy – we cannot find satisfaction.

Desire is infinite. Its fulfilment is very limited.. There is no end to our desires; but when we go to fulfil them, the difficulty comes. It has been so with the most primitive minds, when their desires were [few]. Even [these] could not be accomplished. Now, with our arts and sciences improved and multiplied, our desires cannot be fulfilled [either]. On the other hand, we are struggling to perfect means for the fulfilment of desires, and the desires are increasing.

The most primitive man naturally wanted help from outside for things which he could not accomplish. ...He desired something, and it could not be obtained. He wanted help from other powers. The most ignorant primitive man and the most cultivated man today, each appealing to God and asking for the fulfilment of some desire, are exactly the same. What difference? [Some people] find a great deal of difference. We are always finding much difference in things when there is no difference at all. Both [the primitive man and the cultivated man] plead to the same [power]. You may call it God or Allah or Jehovah. Human beings want something and cannot get it by their own powers, and are after someone who will help them. This is primitive, and it is still present with us. ... We are all born savages and gradually civilise ourselves. ... All of us here, if we search, will find the same fact. Even now this fear does not leave us. We may talk big, become philosophers and all that; but when the blow comes, we find that we must beg for help. We believe in all the superstitions that ever existed. [But] there is no superstition in the world [that does not have some basis of truth]. If I cover my face and only the tip of my [nose] is showing, still it is a bit of my face. So [with] the superstitions – the little bits are true.

You see, the lowest sort of manifestation of religion came with the burial of the departed. ... First they wrapped them up and put them in mounds, and the spirits of the departed came and lived in the [mounds, at night]. ... Then they began to bury them. ... At the gate stands a terrible goddess with a thousand teeth. ... Then [came] the burning of the body and the flames bore the spirit up. ... The Egyptians brought food and water for the departed.

The next great idea was that of the tribal gods. This tribe had one god and that tribe another. The

Jews had their God Jehovah, who was their own tribal god and fought against all the other gods and tribes. That god would do anything to please his own people. If he killed a whole tribe not protected by him, that was all right, quite good. A little love was given, but that love was confined to a small section.

Gradually, higher ideals came. The chief of the conquering tribe was the Chief of chiefs, God of gods. ... So with the Persians when they conquered Egypt. The Persian emperor was the Lord of [lords], and before the emperor nobody could stand. Death was the penalty for anyone who looked at the Persian emperor.

Then came the ideal of God Almighty and All-powerful, the omnipotent, omniscient Ruler of the universe: He lives in heaven, and man pays special tribute to his Most Beloved, who creates everything for man. The whole world is for man. The sun and moon and stars are [for him]. All who have those ideas are primitive men, not civilised and not cultivated at all. All the superior religions had their growth between the Ganga and the Euphrates. ... Outside of India we will find no further development [of religion beyond this idea of God in heaven]. That was the highest knowledge ever obtained outside of India. There is the local heaven where he is and [where] the faithful shall go when they die. ... As far as I have seen, we should call it a very primitive idea. ... Mumbo jumbo in Africa [and] God in heaven – the same. He moves the world, and of course his will is being done everywhere. ...

The old Hebrew people did not care for any heaven. That is one of the reasons they [opposed] Jesus of Nazareth – because he taught life after death. Paradise in Sanskrit means land beyond this life. So the paradise was to make up for all this evil. The primitive man does not care [about] evil. ... He never questions why there should be any. ...

... The word devil is a Persian word. ... The Persians and Hindus [share the Aryan ancestry] upon religious grounds, and ... they spoke the same language, only the words one sect uses for good the other uses for bad. The word Deva is an old Sanskrit word for God, the same word in the Aryan languages. Here the word means the devil. ...

Later on, when man developed [his inner life], he began to question, and to say that God is good. The Persians said that there were two gods – one was bad and one was good. [Their idea was that] everything in this life was good: beautiful country, where there was spring almost the whole year round and nobody died; there was no disease, everything was fine. Then came this Wicked One, and he touched the land, and then came death and disease and mosquitoes and tigers and lions. Then the Aryans left their fatherland and migrated southward. The old Aryans must have lived way to the north. The Jews learnt it [the idea of the devil] from the Persians. The Persians also taught that there will come a day when this wicked god will be killed, and it is our duty to stay with the good god and add our force to him in this eternal struggle between him and the wicked one. ... The whole world will be burnt out and everyone will get a new body.

The Persian idea was that even the wicked will be purified and not be bad any more. The nature of the Aryan was love and poetry. They cannot think of their being burnt [for eternity]. They will all receive new bodies. Then no more death. So that is the best about [religious] ideas outside of India. ...

Along with that is the ethical strain. All that man has to do is to take care of three things: good thought, good word, good deed. That is all. It is a practical, wise religion. Already there has come a little poetry in it. But there is higher poetry and higher thought.

In India we see this Satan in the most ancient part of the Vedas. He just (appears) and immediately disappears. ... In the Vedas the bad god got a blow and disappeared. He is gone, and the Persians took him. We are trying to make him leave the world [al] together. Taking the Persian idea, we are going to make a decent gentleman of him; give him a new body. There was the end of the Satan idea in India.

But the idea of God went on; but mind you, here comes another fact. The idea of God grew side by side with the idea of [materialism] until you have traced it up to the emperor of Persia. But on the other hand comes in metaphysics, philosophy. There is another line of thought, the idea of [the non-dual Âtman, man's] own soul. That also grows. So, outside of India ideas about God had to remain in that concrete form until India came to help them out a bit. ... The other nations stopped with that old concrete idea. In this country [America], there are millions who believe that God is [has?] a body. ... Whole sects say it. [They believe that] He rules the world, but there is a place where He has a body. He sits upon a throne. They light candles and sing songs just as they do in our temples.

But in India they are sensible enough never to make [their God a physical being]. You never see in India a temple of Brahmâ. Why? Because the idea of the soul always existed. The Hebrew race never questioned about the soul. There is no soul idea in the Old Testament at all. The first is in the New Testament. The Persians, they became so practical – wonderfully practical people – a fighting, conquering race. They were the English people of the old time, always fighting and destroying their neighbours – too much engaged in that sort of thing to think about the soul. ...

The oldest idea of [the] soul [was that of] a fine body inside this gross one. The gross one disappears and the fine one appears. In Egypt that fine one also dies, and as soon as the gross body disintegrates, the fine one also disintegrates. That is why they built those pyramids [and embalmed the dead bodies of their ancestors, thus hoping to secure immortality for the departed]

The Indian people have no regard for the dead body at all. [Their attitude is:] "Let us take it and burn it." The son has to set fire to his father's body.

There are two sorts of races, the divine and the demonic. The divine think that they are soul and spirit. The demonic think that they are bodies. The old Indian philosophers tried to insist that the body is nothing. "As a man emits his old garment and takes a new one, even so the old body is [shed] and he takes a new one" (Gita, II. 22). In my case, all my surrounding and education were trying to [make me] the other way. I was always associated with Mohammedans and Christians, who take more care of the body. ...

It is only one step from [the body] to the spirit. ... [In India] they became insistent on this ideal of the soul. It became [synonymous with] the idea of God. ... If the idea of the soul begins to expand, [man must arrive at the conclusion that it is beyond name and form]. ... The Indian idea is that the soul is formless. Whatever is form must break some time or other. There cannot be any form unless it is the result of force and matter; and all combinations must dissolve. If such is the case, [if] your soul is [made of name and form, it disintegrates], and you die, and you are no more immortal. If it is double, it has form and it belongs to nature and it obeys nature's laws of birth and death. ... They find that this [soul] is not the mind ... neither a double.

Thoughts can be guided and controlled. ... [The Yogis of India] practiced to see how far the thoughts can be guided and controlled. By dint of hard work, thoughts may be silenced altogether. If thoughts were [the real man], as soon as thought ceases, he ought to die. Thought ceases in meditation; even the mind's elements are quite quiet. Blood circulation stops. His breath stops, but he is not dead. If thought were he, the whole thing ought to go, but they find it does not go. That is practical [proof]. They came to the conclusion that even mind and thought were not the real man. Then speculation showed that it could not be.

I come, I think and talk. In the midst of all [this activity is] this unity [of the Self]. My thought and action are varied, many [fold] ... but in and through them runs ... that one unchangeable One. It cannot be the body. That is changing every minute. It cannot be the mind; new and fresh thoughts [come] all the time. It is neither the body nor the mind. Both body and mind belong to nature and must obey nature's laws. A free mind never will. ...

Now, therefore, this real man does not belong to nature. It is the person whose mind and body belong to nature. So much of nature we are using. Just as you come to use the pen and ink and chair, so he uses so much of nature in fine and in gross form; gross form, the body, and fine form, the mind. If it is simple, it must be formless. In nature alone are forms. That which is not of nature cannot have any forms, fine or gross. It must be formless. It must be omnipresent. Understand this. [Take] this glass on the table. The glass is form and the table is form. So much of the glass-ness goes off, so much of table-ness [when they break]. ...

The soul ... is nameless because it is formless. It will neither go to heaven nor [to hell] any more than it will enter this glass. It takes the form of the vessel it fills. If it is not in space, either of two things is possible. Either the [soul permeates] space or space is in [it]. You are in space and must have a form. Space limits us, binds us, and makes a form of us. If you are not in space, space is in you. All the heavens and the world are in the person. ...

So it must be with God. God is omnipresent. "Without hands [he grasps] everything; without feet he can move. ... " (Shvetâshvatara Upanishad, III. 19.) He [is] the formless, the deathless, the eternal. The idea of God came. ... He is the Lord of souls, just as my soul is the [lord] of my body. If my soul left the body, the body would not be for a moment. If He left my soul, the soul would not exist. He is the creator of the universe; of everything that dies He is the destroyer. His shadow is death; His shadow is life.

[The ancient Indian philosophers] thought: ... This filthy world is not fit for man's attention. There is nothing in the universe that is [permanent – neither good nor evil].

I told you ... Satan ... did not have much chance [in India]. Why? Because they were very bold in religion. They were not babies. Have you seen that characteristic of children? They are always trying to throw the blame on someone else. Baby minds [are] trying, when they make a mistake, to throw the blame upon someone [else]. On the one hand, we say, "Give me this; give me that." On the other hand, we say, "I did not do this; the devil tempted me. The devil did it." That is the history of mankind, weak mankind. ...

Why is evil? Why is [the world] the filthy, dirty hole? We have made it. Nobody is to blame. We put our hand in the fire. The Lord bless us, [man gets] just what he deserves. Only He is merciful. If we pray to Him, He helps us. He gives Himself to us.

That is their idea. They are [of a] poetic nature. They go crazy over poetry. Their philosophy is poetry. This philosophy is a poem. ... All [high thought] in the Sanskrit is written in poetry. Metaphysics, astronomy – all in poetry.

We are responsible, and how do we come to mischief? [You may say], "I was born poor and miserable. I remember the hard struggle all my life." Philosophers say that you are to blame. You do not mean to say that all this sprang up without any cause whatever? You are a rational being. Your life is not without cause, and you are the cause. You manufacture your own life all the time. ... You make and mould your own life. You are responsible for yourself. Do not lay the blame upon anybody, any Satan. You will only get punished a little more. ...

[A man] is brought up before God, and He says, "Thirty-one stripes for you," ... when comes another man. He says, "Thirty stripes: fifteen for that fellow, and fifteen for the teacher – that awful man who taught him." That is the awful thing in teaching. I do not know what I am going to get. I go all over the world. If I have to get fifteen for each one I have taught!...

We have to come to this idea: "This My Mâyâ is divine." It is My activity [My] divinity. "[My Maya] is hard to cross, but those that take refuge in me [go beyond maya]." (Gita, VII. 14.) But you find out that it is very difficult to cross this ocean [of Maya by] yourself. You cannot. It is the old question - hen and egg. If you do any work, that work becomes the cause and produces the effect. That effect [again] becomes the cause and produces the effect. And so on. If you push this down, it never stops. Once you set a thing in motion, there is no more stopping. I do some work, good or bad, [and it sets up a chain reaction].... I cannot stop now.

It is impossible for us to get out from this bondage [by ourselves]. It is only possible if there is someone more powerful than this law of causation, and if he takes mercy on us and drags us out.

And we declare that there is such a one - God. There is such a being, all merciful.... If there is a God, then it is possible for me to be saved. How can you be saved by your own will? Do you see the philosophy of the doctrine of salvation by grace? You Western people are wonderfully clever, but when you undertake to explain philosophy, you are so wonderfully complicated. How can you save yourself by work, if by salvation you mean that you will be taken out of all this nature? Salvation means just standing upon God, but if you understand what is meant by salvation, then you are the Self.... You are not nature. You are the only thing outside of souls and gods and nature. These are the external existences, and God [is] interpenetrating both nature and soul.

Therefore, just as my soul is [to] my body, we, as it were, are the bodies of God. God-souls-nature – it is one. The One, because, as I say, I mean the body, soul, and mind. But, we have seen, the law of causation pervades every bit of nature, and once you have got caught you cannot get out. When once you get into the meshes of law, a possible way of escape is not [through work done] by you. You can build hospitals for every fly and flea that ever lived.... All this you may do, but it would never lead to salvation.... [Hospitals] go up and they come down again. [Salvation] is only possible if there is some being whom nature never caught, who is the Ruler of nature. He rules nature instead of being ruled by nature. He wills law instead of being downed by law. ... He exists and he is all merciful. The moment you seek Him [He will save you].

Why has He not taken us out? You do not want Him. You want everything but Him. The moment you want Him, that moment you get Him. We never want Him. We say, "Lord, give me a fine house." We want the house, not Him. "Give me health! Save me from this difficulty!"

When a man wants nothing but Him, [he gets Him]. "The same love which wealthy men have for gold and silver and possessions, Lord, may I have the same love for Thee. I want neither earth nor heaven, nor beauty nor learning. I do not want salvation. Let me go to hell again and again. But one thing I want: to love Thee, and for love's sake – not even for heaven."

Whatever man desires, he gets. If you always dream of having a body, [you will get another body]. When this body goes away he wants another, and goes on begetting body after body. Love matter and you become matter. You first become animals. When I see a dog gnawing a bone, I say, "Lord help us!"

Love body until you become dogs and cats! Still degenerate, until you become minerals – all body and nothing else

There are other people, who would have no compromise. The road to salvation is through truth. That was another watchword.

[Man began to progress spiritually] when he kicked the devil out. He stood up and took the responsibility of the misery of the world upon his own shoulders. But whenever he looked [at the] past and future and [at the] law of causation, he knelt down and said, "Lord, save me, [thou] who [art] our creator, our father, and dearest friend." That is poetry, but not very good poetry, I think. Why not? It is the painting of the Infinite [no doubt]. You have it in every language how they paint the Infinite. [But] it is the infinite of the senses, of the muscles.

"[Him] the sun [does not illumine], nor the moon, nor the stars, [nor] the flash of lightning." (Katha Upanishad, II. ii. 15.) That is another painting of the Infinite, by negative language. ... And the last Infinite is painted in [the] spirituality of the Upanishads. Not only is Vedanta the highest philosophy in the world, but it is the greatest poem....

Mark today, this is the ... difference between the first part of the Vedas and the second. In the first, it is all in [the domain of] sense. But all religions are only [concerned with the] infinite of the external world – nature and nature's God.... [Not so Vedanta]. This is the first light that the human mind throws back [of] all that. No satisfaction [comes] of the infinite [in] space. "[The] Self-exisent [One] has [created] the [senses as turned] ... to the outer world. Those therefore who [seek] outside will never find that [which is within]. There are the few who, wanting to know the truth, turn their eyes inward and in their own souls behold the glory [of the Self]." (Katha Upanishad, II. i. 1.)

It is not the infinite of space, but the real Infinite, beyond space, beyond time.... Such is the world missed by the Occident.... Their minds have been turned to external nature and nature's God. Look within yourself and find the truth that you had [forgotten]. Is it possible for mind to come out of this dream without the help of the gods? Once you start the action, there is no help unless the merciful Father takes us out.

That would not be freedom, [even] at the hands of the merciful God. Slavery is slavery. The chain of gold is quite as bad as the chain of iron. Is there a way out?

You are not bound. No one was ever bound. [The Self] is beyond. It is the all. You are the One; there are no two. God was your own reflection cast upon the screen of Maya. The real God [is the Self]. He [whom man] ignorantly worships is that reflection. [They say that] the Father in heaven is God. Why God? [It is because He is] your own reflection that [He] is God. Do you see how you are seeing God all the time? As you unfold yourself, the reflection grows [clearer].

"Two beautiful birds are there sitting upon the same tree. The one [is] calm, silent, majestic; the one below [the individual self], is eating the fruits, sweet and bitter, and becoming happy and sad. [But when the individual self beholds the worshipful Lord as his own true Self, he grieves no more.]" (Mundaka Upanishad, III. i. 1-2.)

... Do not say "God". Do not say "Thou". Say "I". The language of [dualism] says, "God, Thou, my Father." The language of [non-dualism] says, "Dearer unto me than I am myself. I would have no name for Thee. The nearest I can use is I....

"God is true. The universe is a dream. Blessed am I that I know this moment that I [have been and] shall be free all eternity; ... that I know that I am worshipping only myself; that no nature, no delusion, had any hold on me. Vanish nature from me, vanish [these] gods; vanish worship; ... vanish superstitions, for I know myself. I am the Infinite. All these – Mrs. So-and-so, Mr. So-and-so, responsibility, happiness, misery – have vanished. I am the Infinite. How can there be death for me, or birth? Whom shall I fear? I am the One. Shall I be afraid of myself? Who is to be afraid of [whom]? I am the one Existence. Nothing else exists. I am everything."

It is only the question of memory [of your true nature], not salvation by work. Do you get salvation? You are [already] free.

Go on saying, "I am free". Never mind if the next moment delusion comes and says, "I am bound." Dehypnotise the whole thing.

[This truth] is first to be heard. Hear it first. Think on it day and night. Fill the mind [with it] day and night: "I am It. I am the Lord of the universe. Never was there any delusion...." Meditate upon it with all the strength of the mind till you actually see these walls, houses, everything, melt away – [until] body, everything, vanishes. "I will stand alone. I am the One." Struggle on! "Who cares! We want to be free; [we] do not want any powers. Worlds we renounce; heavens we renounce; hells we renounce. What do I care about all these powers, and this and that! What do I care if the mind is controlled or uncontrolled! Let it run on. What of that! I am not the mind, Let it go on!"

The sun [shines on the just and on the unjust]. Is he touched by the defective [character] of anyone? "I am He. Whatever [my] mind does, I am not touched. The sun is not touched by shining on filthy places, I am Existence."

This is the religion of [non-dual] philosophy. [It is] difficult. Struggle on! Down with all superstitions! Neither teachers nor scriptures nor gods [exist]. Down with temples, with priests, with gods, with incarnations, with God himself! I am all the God that ever existed! There, stand up philosophers! No fear! Speak no more of God and [the] superstition of the world. Truth alone triumphs, and this is true. I am the Infinite.

All religious superstitions are vain imaginations. ... This society, that I see you before me, and [that] I am talking to you – this is all superstition; all must be given up. Just see what it takes to become a philosopher! This is the [path] of [Jnâna-] Yoga, the way through knowledge. The other [paths] are easy, slow, ... but this is pure strength of mind. No weakling [can follow this path of knowledge. You must be able to say:] "I am the Soul, the ever free; [I] never was bound. Time is in me, not I in time. God was born in my mind. God the Father, Father of the universe – he is created by me in my own mind...."

Do you call yourselves philosophers? Show it! Think of this, talk [of] this, and [help] each other in this path, and give up all superstition!

❑

Practical Religion: Breathing and Meditation

This article was recorded by Ida Ansell in shorthand. As, however, Swamiji's speed was too great for her in her early days, dots are put in the articles to indicate the omissions, while the words within square brackets are added by way of linking up the disconnected parts.

(Delivered in San Francisco, April 5, 1900)

Everyone's idea of practical religion is according to his theory of practicality and the standpoint he starts from. There is work. There is the system of worship. There is knowledge.

The philosopher thinks ... the difference between bondage and freedom is only caused by knowledge and ignorance. To him, knowledge is the goal, and his practicality is gaining that knowledge.... The worshipper's practical religion is the power of love and devotion. The worker's practical religion consists in doing good works. And so, as in every other thing, we are always trying to ignore the standard of another, trying to bind the whole world to our standard.

Doing good to his fellow-beings is the practical religion of the man full of love. If men do not help to build hospitals, he thinks that they have no religion at all. But there is no reason why everyone should do that. The philosopher, in the same way, may denounce every man who does not have knowledge. People may build twenty thousand hospitals, and the philosopher declares they are but ... the beasts of burden of the gods. The worshipper has his own idea and standard: Men who cannot love God are no good, whatever work they do. The [Yogi believes in] psychic [control and] the conquest of [internal] nature. "How much have you gained towards that? How much control over your senses, over your body?"— that is all the Yogi asks. And, as we said, each one judges the others by his own standard. Men may have given millions of dollars and fed rats and cats, as some do in India. They say that men can take care of themselves, but the poor animals cannot. That is their idea. But to the

Yogi the goal is conquest of [internal] nature, and he judges man by that standard....

We are always talking [about] practical religion. But it must be practical in our sense. Especially [so] in the Western countries. The Protestants' ideal is good works. They do not care much for devotion and philosophy. They think there is not much in it. "What is your knowledge!"

[they say]. "Man has to do something!"

... A little humanitarianism! The churches rail day and night against callous agnosticism. Yet they seem to be veering rapidly towards just that. Callous slaves! Religion of utility! That is the spirit just now. And that is why some Buddhists have become so popular in the West. People do not know whether there is a God or not, whether there is a soul or not. [They think :] This world is full of misery. Try to help this world.

The Yoga doctrine, which we are having our lecture on, is not from that standpoint. [It teaches that] there is the soul, and inside this soul is all power. It is already there, and if we can master this body, all the power will be unfolded. All knowledge is in the soul. Why are people struggling? To lessen the misery.... All unhappiness is caused by our not having mastery over the body.... We are all putting the cart before the horse.... Take the system of work, for instance. We are trying to do good by ... comforting the poor. We do not get to the cause which created the misery. It is like taking a bucket to empty out the ocean, and more [water] comes all the time. The Yogi sees that this is nonsense. [He says that] the way out of misery is to know the cause of misery first.... We try to do the good we can. What for? If there is an incurable disease, why should we struggle and take care of ourselves? If the utilitarians say: "Do not bother about soul and God!"

what is that to the Yogi and what is it to the world? The world does not derive any good [from such an attitude]. More and more misery is going on all the time....

The Yogi says you are to go to the root of all this. Why is there misery in the world? He answers: "It is all our own foolishness, not having proper mastery of our own bodies. That is all." He advises the means by which this misery can be [overcome]. If you can thus get mastery of your body, all the misery of the world will vanish. Every hospital is praying that more and more sick people will come there. Every time you think of doing some charity, you think there is some beggar to take your charity. If you say, "O Lord, let the world be full of charitable people!"

– you mean, let the world be full of beggars also. Let the world be full of good works - let the world be full of misery. This is out-and-out slavishness!

... The Yogi says, religion is practical if you know first why misery exists. All the misery in the world is in the senses. Is there any ailment in the sun, moon, and stars? The same fire that cooks your meal burns the child. Is it the fault of the fire? Blessed be the fire! Blessed be this electricity! It gives light.... Where can you lay the blame? Not on the elements. The world is neither good nor bad; the world is the world. The fire is the fire. If you burn your finger in it, you are a fool. If you [cook your meal and with it satisfy your hunger,] you are a wise man. That is all the difference. Circumstances can never be good or bad. Only the individual man can be good or bad. What is meant by the world being good or bad? Misery and happiness can only belong to the sensuous individual man.

The Yogis say that nature is the enjoyed; the soul is the enjoyer. All misery and happiness – where is it? In the senses. It is the touch of the senses that causes pleasure and pain, heat and cold. If we can control the senses and order what they shall feel – not let them order us about as they are doing now – if they can obey our commands, become our servants, the problem is solved at once. We are bound by the senses; they play upon us, make fools of us all the time.

Here is a bad odour. It will bring me unhappiness as soon as it touches my nose. I am the slave of my nose. If I am not its slave, I do not care. A man curses me. His curses enter my ears and are retained in my mind and body. If I am the master, I shall say: "Let these things go; they are nothing to me. I am not miserable. I do not bother." This is the outright, pure, simple, clear-cut truth.

The other problem to be solved is – is it practical? Can man attain to the power of mastery of the body? ... Yoga says it is practical .... Supposing it is not – suppose there are doubts in your mind. You have got to try it. There is no other way out....

You may do good works all the time. All the same, you will be the slave of your senses, you will be miserable and unhappy. You may study the philosophy of every religion. Men in this country carry loads and loads of books on their backs. They are mere scholars, slaves of the senses, and therefore happy and unhappy. They read two thousand books, and that is all right; but as soon as a little misery comes, they are worried, anxious.... You call yourselves men! You stand up ... and build hospitals. You are fools!

What is the difference between men and animals? ... "Food and [sleep], procreation of the species, and fear exist in common with the animals. There is one difference: Man can control all these and become God, the master." Animals cannot do it. Animals can do charitable work. Ants do it. Dogs do it. What is the difference then? Men can be masters of themselves.

They can resist the reaction to anything.... The animal cannot resist anything. He is held ... by the string of nature everywhere. That is all the distinction. One is the master of nature, the other the slave of nature. What is nature? The five senses....

[The conquest of internal nature] is the only way out, according to Yoga.... The thirst for God is religion.... Good works and all that [merely] make the mind a little quiet. To practice this – to be perfect – all depends upon our past. I have been studying [Yoga] all my life and have made very little progress yet. But I have got enough [result] to believe that this is the only true way. The day will come when I will be master of myself. If not in this life, [in another life]. I will struggle and never let go. Nothing is lost. If I die this moment, all my past struggles [will come to my help]. Have you not seen what makes the difference between one man and another? It is their past. The past habits make one man a genius and another man a fool. You may have the power of the past and can succeed in five minutes. None can predict the moment of time. We all have to attain [perfection] some time or other.

The greater part of the practical lessons which the Yogi gives us is in the mind, the power of concentration and meditation.... We have become so materialistic. When we think of ourselves, we find only the body. The body has become the ideal, nothing else. Therefore a little physical help is necessary....

First, to sit in the posture In which you can sit still for a long time. All the nerve currents which are working pass along the spine. The spine is not intended to support the weight of the body. Therefore the posture must be such that the weight of the body is not on the spine. Let it be free from all pressure.

There are some other preliminary things. There is the great question of food and exercise....

The food must be simple and taken several times [a day] instead of once or twice. Never get very hungry. "He who eats too much cannot be a Yogi. He who fasts too much cannot be a Yogi. He who sleeps too much cannot be a Yogi, nor he who keeps awake too much." (Gita, VI. 16.) He who does not do any work and he who works too hard cannot succeed. Proper food, proper exercise, proper sleep, proper wakefulness – these are necessary for any success.

What the proper food is, what kind, we have to determine ourselves. Nobody can determine that [for us]. As a general practice, we have to shun exciting food.... We do not know how to vary our diet with our occupation. We always forget that it is the food out of which we manufacture everything we have. So the amount and kind of energy that we want, the food must determine....

Violent exercises are not all necessary.... If you want to be muscular, Yoga is not for you. You have to manufacture a finer organism than you have now. Violent exercises are positively hurtful.... Live amongst those who do not take too much exercise. If you do not take violent exercise, you will live longer. You do not want to burn out your lamp in muscles! People who work with their brains are the longest-lived people.... Do not burn the lamp quickly. Let it burn slowly and gently.... Every anxiety, every violent exercise – physical and mental – [means] you are burning the lamp.

The proper diet means, generally, simply do not eat highly spiced foods. There are three sorts of mind, says the Yogi, according to the elements of nature. One is the dull mind, which covers the luminosity of the soul. Then there is that which makes people active, and lastly, that which makes them calm and peaceful.

Now there are persons born with the tendency to sleep all the time. Their taste will be towards that type of food which is rotting – crawling cheese. They will eat cheese that fairly jumps off the table. It is a natural tendency with them.

Then active people. Their taste is for everything hot and pungent, strong alcohol....

Sâttvika people are very thoughtful, quiet, and patient. They take food in small quantities, and never anything bad.

I am always asked the question: "Shall I give up meat?" My Master said, "Why should you give up anything? It will give you up." Do not give up anything in nature. Make it so hot for nature that she will give you up. There will come a time when you cannot possibly eat meat. The very sight of it will disgust you. There will come a time when many things you are struggling to give up will be distasteful, positively loathsome.

Then there are various sorts of breathing exercises. One consists of three parts: the drawing in of the breath, the holding of the breath – stopping still without breathing – and throwing the breath out. [Some breathing exercises] are rather difficult, and some of the complicated ones are attended with great danger if done without proper diet. I would not advise you to go through any one of these except the very simple ones.

Take a deep breath and fill the lungs. Slowly throw the breath out. Take it through one nostril and fill the lungs, and throw it out slowly through the other nostril. Some of us do not breathe deeply enough. Others cannot fill the lungs enough. These breathings will correct that very much. Half an hour in the morning and half an hour in the evening will make you another person. This sort of breathing is never dangerous. The other exercises should be practiced very slowly. And measure your strength. If ten minutes are a drain, only take five.

The Yogi is expected to keep his own body well. These various breathing exercises are a great help in regulating the different parts of the body. All the different parts are inundated with breath. It is through breath that we gain control of them all. Disharmony in parts of the body is controlled by more flow of the nerve currents towards them. The Yogi ought to be able to tell when in any part pain is caused by less vitality or more. He has to equalise that....

Another condition [for success in Yoga] is chastity. It is the corner-stone of all practice. Married or unmarried – perfect chastity. It is a long subject, of course, but I want to tell you: Public discussions of this subject are not to the taste of this country. These Western countries are full of the most degraded beings in the shape of teachers who teach men and women that if they are chaste they will be hurt. How do they gather all this? ... People come to me – thousands come every year – with this one question. Someone has told them that if they are chaste and pure they will be hurt physically.... How do these teachers know it? Have they been chaste? Those unchaste, impure fools, lustful creatures, want to drag the whole world down to their [level]!

Nothing is gained except by sacrifice.... The holiest function of our human consciousness, the noblest, do not make it unclean! Do not degrade it to the level of the brutes.... Make yourselves decent men! ... Be chaste and pure! ... There is no other way. Did Christ find any other way? ... If you can conserve and use the energy properly, it leads you to God. Inverted, it is hell itself ....

It is much easier to do anything upon the external plane, but the greatest conqueror in the world finds himself a mere child when he tries to control his own mind. This is the world he has to conquer – the greater and more difficult world to conquer. Do not despair! Awake, arise, and stop not until the goal is reached!

❑

The Gita I

This article was recorded by Ida Ansell in shorthand. As, however, Swamiji's speed was too great for her in her early days, dots are put in the articles to indicate the omissions, while the words within square brackets are added by way of linking up the disconnected parts.

(Delivered in San Francisco, on May 26, 1900)

To understand the Gita requires its historical background. The Gita is a commentary on the Upanishads. The Upanishads are the Bible of India. They occupy the same place as the New Testament does. There are [more than] a hundred books comprising the Upanishads, some very small and some big, each a separate treatise. The Upanishads do not reveal the life of any teacher, but simply teach principles. They are [as it were] shorthand notes taken down of discussion in [learned assemblies], generally in the courts of kings. The word Upanishad may mean "sittings" [or "sitting near a teacher"]. Those of you who may have studied some of the Upanishads can understand how they are condensed shorthand sketches. After long discussions had been held, they were taken down, possibly from memory. The difficulty is that you get very little of the background. Only the luminous points are mentioned there. The origin of ancient Sanskrit is 5000 B.C.; the Upanishads [are at least] two thousand years before that. Nobody knows [exactly] how old they are. The Gita takes the ideas of the Upanishads and in [some] cases the very words. They are strung together with the idea of bringing out, in a compact, condensed, and systematic form, the whole subject the Upanishads deal with.

The [original] scriptures of the Hindus are called the Vedas. They were so vast – the mass of writings – that if the texts alone were brought here, this room would not contain them. Many of them are lost. They were divided into branches, each branch put into the head of certain priests and kept alive by memory. Such men still exist. They will repeat book after book of the Vedas without missing a single intonation. The larger portion of the Vedas has disappeared. The small portion left makes a whole library by itself. The oldest of these contains the hymns of the Rig-Veda. It is the aim of the modern scholar to restore [the sequence of the Vedic compositions]. The old, orthodox idea is quite different, as your orthodox idea of the Bible is quite different from the modern scholar's. The Vedas are divided into two portions: one the Upanishads, the philosophical portion, the other the work portion.

We will try to give a little idea of the work portion. It consists of rituals and hymns, various hymns addressed to various gods. The ritual portion is composed of ceremonies, some of them very elaborate. A great many priests are required. The priestly function became a science by itself, owing to the elaboration of the ceremonials. Gradually the popular idea of veneration grew round these hymns and rituals. The gods disappeared and in their place were left the rituals. That was the curious development in India. The orthodox Hindu [the Mimâmsaka] does not believe in gods, the unorthodox believe in them. If you ask the orthodox Hindu what the meaning is of these gods in the Vedas, [he will not be able to give any satisfactory answer]. The priests sing these hymns and pour libations and offering into the fire. When you ask the orthodox Hindu the meaning of this, he says that words have the power to produce certain effects. That is all. There is all the natural and supernatural power that ever existed.

The Vedas are simply words that have the mystical power to produce effects if the sound intonation is right. If one sound is wrong it will not do. Each one must be perfect. [Thus] what in other religions is called prayer disappeared and the Vedas became the gods. So you see the tremendous importance that was attached to the words of the Vedas. These are the eternal words out of which the whole universe has been produced. There cannot be any thought without the word. Thus whatever there is in this world is the manifestation of thought, and thought can only manifest itself through words. This mass of words by which the unmanifested thought becomes manifest, that is what is meant by the Vedas. It follows that the external existence of everything [depends on the Vedas, for thought] does not exist without the word. If the word "horse" did not exist, none could think of a horse. [So] there must be [an intimate relation between] thought, word, and the external object. What are these words [in reality]? The Vedas. They do not call it Sanskrit language at all. It is Vedic language, a divine language. Sanskrit is a degenerate form. So are all other languages. There is no language older than Vedic. You may ask, "Who wrote the Vedas?" They were not written. The words are the Vedas. A word is Veda, if I can pronounce it rightly. Then it will immediately produce the [desired] effect.

This mass of Vedas eternally exists and all the world is the manifestation of this mass of words.

Then when the cycle ends, all this manifestation of energy becomes finer and finer, becomes only words, then thought. In the next cycle, first the thought changes into words and then out of those words [the whole universe] is produced. If there is something here that is not in the Vedas, that is your delusion. It does not exist.

[Numerous] books upon that subject alone defend the Vedas. If you tell [their authors] that the Vedas must have been pronounced by men first, [they will simply laugh]. You never heard of any [man uttering them for the first time]. Take Buddha's words. There is a tradition that he lived and spoke these words [many times before]. If the Christian stands up and says, "My religion is a historical religion and therefore yours is wrong and ours is true," [the Mimamsaka replies], "Yours being historical, you confess that a man invented it nineteen hundred years ago. That which is true must be infinite and eternal. That is the one test of truth. It never decays, it is always the same. You confess your religion was created by such-and-such a man. The Vedas were not. By no prophets or anything. ... Only infinite words, infinite by their very nature, from which the whole universe comes and goes." In the abstract it is perfectly correct. ... The sound must be the beginning of creation. There must be germ sounds like germ plasm. There cannot be any ideas without the words. ... Wherever there are sensations, ideas, emotions, there must be words.

The difficulty is when they say that these four books are the Vedas and nothing else. [Then] the Buddhist will stand up and say, "Ours are Vedas. They were revealed to us later on." That cannot be. Nature does not go on in that way. Nature does not manifest her laws bit by bit, an inch of gravitation today and [another inch] tomorrow. No, every law is complete. There is no evolution in law at all. It is [given] once and for ever. It is all nonsense, this "new religion and better inspiration," and all that. It means nothing. There may be a hundred thousand laws and man may know only a few today. We discover them – that is all. Those old priests with their tremendous [claims about eternal words], having dethroned the gods, took the place of the gods. [They said], "You do not understand the power of words. We know how to use them. We are the living gods of the world. Pay us; we will manipulate the words, and you will get what you want. Can you pronounce the words yourself? You cannot, for, mind you, one mistake will produce the opposite effect. You want to be rich, handsome, have a long life, a fine husband?" Only pay the priest and keep quiet!

Yet there is another side. The ideal of the first part of the Vedas is entirely different from the ideal of the other part, the Upanishads. The ideal of the first part coincides with [that of] all other religions of the world except the Vedanta. The ideal is enjoyment here and hereafter – man and wife, husband and children. Pay your dollar, and the priest will give you a certificate, and you will have a happy time afterwards in heaven. You will find all your people there and have this merry-go-round without end. No tears, no weeping – only laughing. No stomach-ache, but yet eating. No headache, but yet [parties]. That, considered the priests, was the highest goal of man.

There is another idea in this philosophy which is according to your modern ideas. Man is a slave of nature, and slave eternally he has got to remain. We call it Karma. Karma means law, and it applies everywhere. Everything is bound by Karma. "Is there no way out?" "No! Remain slaves all through the years – fine slaves. We will manipulate the words so that you will only have the good and not the bad side of all – if you will pay [us] enough." That was the ideal of [the Mimamsakas]. These are the ideals which are popular throughout the ages. The vast mass of mankind are never thinkers. Even if they try to think, the [effect of the] vast mass of superstitions on them is terrible. The moment they weaken, one blow comes, and the backbone breaks into twenty pieces. They can only be moved by lures and threats. They can never move of their own accord. They must be frightened, horrified, or terrorised, and they are your slaves for ever. They have nothing else to do but to pay and obey. Everything else is done by the priest. ... How much easier religion becomes! You see, you have nothing to do. Go home and sit quietly. Somebody is doing the whole thing for you. Poor, poor animals!

Side by side, there was the other system. The Upanishads are diametrically opposite in all their conclusions. First of all, the Upanishads believe in God, the creator of the universe, its ruler. You find later on [the idea of a benign Providence]. It is an entirely opposite [conception]. Now, although we hear the priest, the ideal is much more subtle. Instead of many gods they made one God.

The second idea, that you are all bound by the law of Karma, the Upanishads admit, but they declare the way out. The goal of man is to go beyond law. And enjoyment can never be the goal, because enjoyment can only be in nature.

In the third place, the Upanishads condemn all the sacrifices and say that is mummery. That may give you all you want, but it is not desirable, for the more you get, the more you [want], and you run round and round in a circle eternally, never getting to the end – enjoying and weeping. Such a thing as eternal happiness is impossible anywhere. It is only a child's dream. The same energy becomes joy and sorrow.

I have changed my psychology a bit today. I have found the most curious fact. You have a certain idea and you do not want to have it, and you think of something else, and the idea you want to suppress is entirely suppressed. What is that idea? I saw it come out in fifteen minutes. It came out and staggered me. It was strong, and it came in such a violent and terrible fashion [that] I thought here was a madman. And when it was over, all that had happened [was a suppression of the previous emotion]. What came out? It was my own bad impression which had to be worked out. "Nature will have her way. What can suppression do?" (Gita, III. 33.) That is a terrible [statement] in the Gita. It seems it may be a vain struggle after all. You may have a hundred thousand [urges competing] at the same time. You may repress [them], but the moment the spring rebounds, the whole thing is there again.

[But there is hope]. If you are powerful enough, you can divide your consciousness into twenty parts all at the same time. I am changing my psychology. Mind grows. That is what the Yogis say. There is one passion and it rouses another, and the first one dies. If you are angry, and then happy, the next moment the anger passes away. Out of that anger you manufactured the next state. These states are always interchangeable. Eternal happiness and misery are a child's dream. The Upanishads point out that the goal of man is neither misery nor happiness, but we have to be master of that out of which these are manufactured. We must be masters of the situation at its very root, as it were.

The other point of divergence is: the Upanishads condemn all rituals, especially those that involve the killing of animals. They declare those all nonsense. One school of old philosophers says that you must kill such an animal at a certain time if the effect is to be produced. [You may reply], "But [there is] also the sin of taking the life of the animal; you will have to suffer for that." They say that is all nonsense. How do you know what is right and what is wrong? Your mind says so? Who cares what your mind says? What nonsense are you talking? You are setting your mind against the scriptures. If your mind says something and the Vedas say something else, stop your mind and believe in the Vedas. If they say, killing a man is right, that is right. If you say, "No, my conscience says [otherwise," it won't do]. The moment you believe in any book as the eternal word, as sacred, no more can you question. I do not see how you people here believe in the Bible whenever you say about [it], "How wonderful those words are, how right and how good!"

Because, if you believe in the Bible as the word of God, you have no right to judge at all. The moment you judge, you think you are higher than the Bible. [Then] what is the use of the Bible to you? The priests say, "We refuse to make the comparison with your Bible or anybody's. It is no use comparing, because – what is the authority? There it ends. If you think something is not right, go and get it right according to the Vedas."

The Upanishads believe in that, [but they have a higher standard too]. On the one hand, they do not want to overthrow the Vedas, and on the other they see these animal sacrifices and the priests stealing everybody's money. But in the psychology they are all alike. All the differences have been in the philosophy, [regarding] the nature of the soul. Has it a body and a mind? And is the mind only a bundle of nerves, the motor nerves and the sensory nerves? Psychology, they all take for granted, is a perfect science. There cannot be any difference there. All the fight has been regarding philosophy – the nature of the soul, and God, and all that.

Then another great difference between the priests and the Upanishads. The Upanishads say, renounce. That is the test of everything. Renounce everything. It is the creative faculty that brings us into all this entanglement. The mind is in its own nature when it is calm. The moment you can calm it, that [very] moment you will know the truth. What is it that is whirling the mind? Imagination, creative activity. Stop creation and you know the truth. All power of creation must stop, and then you know the truth at once.

On the other hand, the priests are all for [creation]. Imagine a species of life [in which there is no creative activity. It is unthinkable]. The people had to have a plan [of evolving a stable society. A system of rigid selection was adopted. For instance,] no people who are blind and halt can be married. [As a result] you will find so much less deformity [in India] than in any other country in the world. Epileptics and insane [people] are very rare [there]. That is owing to direct selection. The priests say, "Let them become Sannyâsins." On the other hand, the Upanishads say, "Oh no, [the] earth's best and finest [and] freshest flowers should be laid upon the altar. The strong, the young, with sound intellect and sound body – they must struggle for the truth."

So with all these divergences of opinion, I have told you that the priests already differentiated themselves into a separate caste. The second is the caste of the kings. ... All the Upanishadic philosophy is from the brains of kings, not priests. There [runs] an economic struggle through every religious struggle. This animal called man has some religious influence, but he is guided by economy. Individuals are guided by something else, but the mass of mankind never made a move unless economy was [involved]. You may [preach a religion that may not be perfect in every detail], but if there is an economic background [to it], and you have the most [ardent champions] to preach it, you can convince a whole country.

Whenever any religion succeeds, it must have economic value. Thousands of similar sects will be struggling for power, but only those who meet the real economic problem will have it. Man is guided by the stomach. He walks and the stomach goes first and the head afterwards. Have you not seen that? It will take ages for the head to go first. By the time a man is sixty years of age, he is called out of [the world]. The whole of life is one delusion, and just when you begin to see things the way they are, you are snatched off. So long as the stomach went first you were all right. When children's dreams begin to vanish and you begin to look at things the way they are, the head goes. Just when the head goes first, [you go out].

[For] the religion of the Upanishads to be popularised was a hard task. Very little economy is there, but tremendous altruism. ...

The Upanishads had very little kingdom, although they were discovered by kings that held all the royal power in their hands. So the struggle ... began to be fiercer. Its culminating point came two thousand years after, in Buddhism. The seed of Buddhism is here, [in] the ordinary struggle between the king and the priest; and [in the struggle] all religion declined. One wanted to sacrifice religion, the other wanted to cling to the sacrifices, to Vedic gods, etc. Buddhism ... broke the chains of the masses. All castes and creeds alike became equal in a minute. So the great religious ideas in India exist, but have yet to be preached: otherwise they do no good. ...

In every country it is the priest who is conservative, for two reasons – because it is his bread and because he can only move with the people. All priests are not strong. If the people say, "Preach two thousand gods," the priests will do it. They are the servants of the congregation who pay them. God does not pay them. So blame yourselves before blaming the priests. You can only get the government and the religion and the priesthood you deserve, and no better.

So the great struggle began in India and it comes to one of its culminating points in the Gita. When it was causing fear that all India was going to be broken up between [the] two ... [groups], there rose this man Krishna, and in the Gita he tries to reconcile the ceremony and the philosophy of the priests and the people. Krishna is loved and worshipped in the same way as you do Christ. The difference is only in the age. The Hindus keep the birthday of Krishna as you do Christ's. Krishna lived five thousand years ago and his life is full of miracles, some of them very similar to those in the life of Christ. The child was born in prison. The father took him away and put him with the shepherds. All children born in that year were ordered to be killed. ... He was killed; that was his fate.

Krishna was a married man. There are thousands of books about him. They do not interest me much. The Hindus are great in telling stories, you see. [If] the Christian missionaries tell one story from their Bible, the Hindus will produce twenty stories. You say the whale swallowed Jonah; the Hindus say someone swallowed an elephant. ... Since I was a child I have heard about Krishna's life. I take it for granted there must have been a man called Krishna, and his Gita shows he has [left] a wonderful book. I told you, you can understand the character of a man by analysing the fables about him. The fables have the nature [of decorations]. You must find they are all polished and manipulated to fit into the character. For instance, take Buddha. The central idea [is] sacrifice. There are thousands of folklore, but in every case the sacrifice must have been kept up. There are thousands of stories about Lincoln, about some characteristic of that great man. You take all the fables and find the general idea and [know] that that was the central character of the man. You find in Krishna that non-attachment is the central idea. He does not need anything. He does not want anything. He works for work's sake. "Work for work's sake. Worship for worship's sake. Do good because it is good to do good. Ask no more." That must have been the character of the man. Otherwise these fables could not be brought down to the one idea of non-attachment. The Gita is not his only sermon. ...

He is the most rounded man I know of, wonderfully developed equally in brain and heart and hand.

Every moment [of his] is alive with activity, either as a gentleman, warrior, minister, or something else. Great as a gentleman, as a scholar, as a poet. This all-rounded and wonderful activity and combination of brain and heart you see in the Gita and other books. Most wonderful heart, exquisite language, and nothing can approach it anywhere. This tremendous activity of the man – the impression is still there. Five thousand years have passed and he has influenced millions and millions. Just think what an influence this man has over the whole world, whether you know it or not. My regard for him is for his perfect sanity. No cobwebs in that brain, no superstition. He knows the use of everything, and when it is necessary to [assign a place to each], he is there. Those that talk, go everywhere, question about the mystery of the Vedas, etc., they do not know the truth. They are no better than frauds. There is a place in the Vedas [even] for superstition, for ignorance. The whole secret is to find out the proper place for everything.

Then that heart! He is the first man, way before Buddha, to open the door of religion to every caste. That wonderful mind! That tremendously active life! Buddha's activity was on one plane, the plane of teaching. He could not keep his wife and child and become a teacher at the same time. Krishna preached in the midst of the battlefield. "He who in the midst of intense activity finds himself in the greatest calmness, and in the greatest peace finds intense activity, that is the greatest [Yogi as well as the wisest man]." (Ibid. IV. 18.) It means nothing to this man – the flying of missiles about him. Calm and sedate he goes on discussing the problems of life and death. Each one of the prophets is the best commentary on his own teaching. If you want to know what is meant by the doctrine of the New Testament, you go to Mr. So-and-so. [But] read again and again [the four Gospels and try to understand their import in the light of the wonderful life of the Master as depicted there]. The great men think, and you and I [also] think. But there is a difference. We think and our bodies do not follow. Our actions do not harmonise with our thoughts. Our words have not the power of the words that become Vedas. ... Whatever they think must be accomplished. If they say, "I do this," the body does it. Perfect obedience. This is the end. You can think yourself God in one minute, but you cannot be [God]. That is the difficulty. They become what they think. We will become [only] by [degrees].

You see, that was about Krishna and his time. In the next lecture we will know more of his book.

❑

The Gita II

This article was recorded by Ida Ansell in shorthand. As, however, Swamiji's speed was too great for her in her early days, dots are put in the articles to indicate the omissions, while the words within square brackets are added by way of linking up the disconnected parts.

(Delivered in San Francisco, on May 28, 1900)

The Gitâ requires a little preliminary introduction. The scene is laid on the battlefield of Kurukshetra. There were two branches of the same race fighting for the empire of India about five thousand years ago. The Pândavas had the right, but the Kauravas had the might. The Pandavas were five brothers, and they were living in a forest. Krishna was the friend of the Pandavas. The Kauravas would not grant them as much land as would cover the point of a needle.

The opening scene is the battlefield, and both sides see their relatives and friends – one brother on one side and another on the other side; a grandfather on one side, grandson on the other side. ... When Arjuna sees his own friends and relatives on the other side and knows that he may have to kill them, his heart gives way and he says that he will not fight. Thus begins the Gita.

For all of us in this world life is a continuous fight. ... Many a time comes when we want to interpret our weakness and cowardice as forgiveness and renunciation. There is no merit in the renunciation of a beggar. If a person who can [give a blow] forbears, there is merit in that. If a person who has, gives up, there is merit in that. We know how often in our lives through laziness and cowardice we give up the battle and try to hypnotise our minds into the belief that we are brave.

The Gita opens with this very significant verse: "Arise, O Prince! Give up this faint-heartedness, this weakness! Stand up and fight!"

(Gita, II. 3.) Then Arjuna, trying to argue the matter [with Krishna], brings higher moral ideas, how non-resistance is better than resistance, and so on. He is trying to justify himself, but he cannot fool Krishna. Krishna is the higher Self, or God. He sees through the argument at once. In this case [the motive] is weakness. Arjuna sees his own relatives and he cannot strike them. ...

There is a conflict in Arjuna's heart between his emotionalism and his duty. The nearer we are to [beasts and] birds, the more we are in the hells of emotion. We call it love. It is self-hypnotisation. We are under the control of our [emotions] like animals. A cow can sacrifice its life for its young. Every animal can. What of that? It is not the blind, birdlike emotion that leads to perfection. ... [To reach] the eternal consciousness, that is the goal of man! There emotion has no place, nor sentimentalism, nor anything that belongs to the senses – only the light of pure reason. [There] man stands as spirit.

Now, Arjuna is under the control of this emotionalism. He is not what he should be – a great self-controlled, enlightened sage working through the eternal light of reason. He has become like an animal, like a baby, just letting his heart carry away his brain, making a fool of himself and trying to cover his weakness with the flowery names of "love" and so on. Krishna sees through that. Arjuna talks like a man of little learning and brings out many reasons, but at the same time he talks the language of a fool.

"The sage is not sorry for those that are living nor for those that die." (Ibid. 11.) [Krishna says :] "You cannot die nor can I. There was never a time when we did not exist. There will never be a time when we shall not exist. As in this life a man begins with childhood, and [passes through youth and old age, so at death he merely passes into another kind of body]. Why should a wise man be sorry?" (Ibid. 12-13.) And where is the beginning of this emotionalism that has got hold of you? It is in the senses. "It is the touch of the senses that brings all this quality of existence: heat and cold, pleasure and pain. They come and go." (Ibid. 14.) Man is miserable this moment, happy the next. As such he cannot experience the nature of the soul. ...

"Existence can never be non-existence, neither can non-existence ever become existence. ... Know, therefore, that that which pervades all this universe is without beginning or end. It is unchangeable. There is nothing in the universe that can change [the Changeless]. Though this body has its beginning and end, the dweller in the body is infinite and without end." (Ibid. 16-18.)

Knowing this, stand up and fight! Not one step back, that is the idea. ... Fight it out, whatever comes. Let the stars move from the sphere! Let the whole world stand against us! Death means only a change of garment. What of it? Thus fight! You gain nothing by becoming cowards. ... Taking a step backward, you do not avoid any misfortune. You have cried to all the gods in the world. Has misery ceased? The masses in India cry to sixty million gods, and still die like dogs. Where are these gods? ... The gods come to help you when you have succeeded. So what is the use? Die game. ... This bending the knee to superstitions, this selling yourself to your own mind does not befit you, my soul. You are infinite, deathless, birthless. Because you are infinite spirit, it does not befit you to be a slave. ... Arise! Awake! Stand up and fight! Die if you must. There is none to help you. You are all the world. Who can help you?

"Beings are unknown to our human senses before birth and after death. It is only in the interim that they are manifest. What is there to grieve about? (Ibid. 28.)

"Some look at It [the Self] with wonder. Some talk of It as wonderful. Others hear of It as wonderful. Others, hearing of It, do not understand." (Ibid. 29.)

But if you say that killing all these people is sinful, then consider this from the standpoint of your own caste-duty. ... "Making pleasure and misery the same, making success and defeat the same, do thou stand up and fight. (Ibid. 38.)

This is the beginning of another peculiar doctrine of the Gita – the doctrine of non-attachment. That is to say, we have to bear the result of our own actions because we attach ourselves to them. ... "Only what is done as duty for duty's sake ... can scatter the bondage of Karma." (Ibid. 39.) There is no danger that you can overdo it. ... "If you do even a little of it, [this Yoga will save you from the terrible round of birth and death]. (Ibid. 40.)

"Know, Arjuna, the mind that succeeds is the mind that is concentrated. The minds that are taken up with two thousand subjects (have) their energies dispersed. Some can talk flowery language and think there is nothing beyond the Vedas. They want to go to heaven. They want good things through the power of the Vedas, and so they make sacrifices." (Ibid. 41-43.) Such will never attain any success [in spiritual life] unless they give up all these materialistic ideas. (Ibid. 44.)

That is another great lesson. Spirituality can never be attained unless all material ideas are given up. ... What is in the senses? The senses are all delusion. People wish to retain them [in heaven] even after they are dead – a pair of eyes, a nose. Some imagine they will have more organs than they have now. They want to see God sitting on a throne through all eternity – the material body of God. ... Such men's desires are for the body, for food and drink and enjoyment. It is the materialistic life prolonged. Man cannot think of anything beyond this life. This life is all for the body. "Such a man never comes to that concentration which leads to freedom." (Ibid. 44.)

"The Vedas only teach things belonging to the three Gunas, to Sattva, Rajas, and Tamas." (Ibid. 45.) The Vedas only teach about things in nature. People cannot think anything they do not see on earth. If they talk about heaven, they think of a king sitting on a throne, of people burning incense. It is all nature, nothing beyond nature. The Vedas, therefore, teach nothing but nature. "Go beyond nature, beyond the dualities of existence, beyond your own consciousness, caring for nothing, neither for good nor for evil." (Ibid. 45.)

We have identified ourselves with our bodies. We are only body, or rather, possessed of a body. If I am pinched, I cry. All this is nonsense, since I am the soul. All this chain of misery, imagination, animals, gods, and demons, everything, the whole world all this comes from the identification of ourselves with the body. I am spirit. Why do I jump if you pinch me? ... Look at the slavery of it. Are you not ashamed? We are religious! We are philosophers! We are sages! Lord bless us! What are we? Living hells, that is what we are. Lunatics, that is what we are!

We cannot give up the idea [of body]. We are earth-bound. ... Our ideas are burial grounds. When we leave the body we are bound by thousands of elements to those [ideas].

Who can work without any attachment? That is the real question. Such a man is the same whether his work succeeds or fails. His heart does not give one false beat even if his whole life-work is burnt to ashes in a moment. “This is the sage who always works for work’s sake without caring for the results. Thus he goes beyond the pain of birth and death. Thus he becomes free.” (Ibid. 51.) Then he sees that this attachment is all delusion. The Self can never be attached. ... Then he goes beyond all the scriptures and philosophies. (Ibid. 52.) If the mind is deluded and pulled into a whirlpool by books and scriptures, what is the good of all these scriptures? One says this, another says that. What book shall you take? Stand alone! See the glory of your own soul, and see that you will have to work. Then you will become a man of firm will. (Ibid. 53.)

Arjuna asks: “Who is a person of established will?” (Ibid. 54.)

[Krishna answers:] “The man who has given up all desires, who desires nothing, not even this life, nor freedom, nor gods, nor work, nor anything. When he has become perfectly satisfied, he has no more cravings.” (Ibid. 55.) He has seen the glory of the Self and has found that the world, and the gods, and heaven are ... within his own Self. Then the gods become no gods; death becomes no death; life becomes no life. Everything has changed. "A man is said to be [illumined] if his will has become firm, if his mind is not disturbed by misery, if he does not desire any happiness, if he is free of all [attachment], of all fear, of all anger. (Ibid. 56.) ...

"As the tortoise can draw in his legs, and if you strike him, not one foot comes out, even so the sage can draw all his sense-organs inside," (Ibid. 58.) and nothing can force them out. Nothing can shake him, no temptation or anything. Let the universe tumble about him, it does not make one single ripple in his mind.

Then comes a very important question. Sometimes people fast for days. ... When the worst man has fasted for twenty days, he becomes quite gentle. Fasting and torturing themselves have been practiced by people all over the world. Krishna's idea is that this is all nonsense. He says that the senses will for the moment recede from the man who tortures himself, but will emerge again with twenty times more [power]. ... What should you do? The idea is to be natural – no asceticism. Go on, work, only mind that you are not attached. The will can never be fixed strongly in the man who has not learnt and practiced the secret of non-attachment.

I go out and open my eyes. If something is there, I must see it. I cannot help it. The mind runs after the senses. Now the senses must give up any reaction to nature.

"Where it is dark night for the [sense-bound] world, the self controlled [man] is awake. It is daylight for him. ... And where the world is awake, the sage sleeps." (Ibid. 69.) Where is the world awake? In the senses. People want to eat and drink and have children, and then they die a dog's death. ... They are always awake for the senses. Even their religion is just for that. They invent a God to help them, to give them more women, more money, more children – never a God to help them become more godlike! "Where the whole world is awake, the sage sleeps. But where the ignorant are asleep, there the sage keeps awake" (Ibid. 69.) – in the world of light where man looks upon himself not as a bird, not as an animal, not as a body, but as infinite spirit, deathless, immortal. There, where the ignorant are asleep, and do not have time, nor intellect, nor power to understand, there the sage is awake. That is daylight for him.

"As all the rivers of the world constantly pour their waters into the ocean, but the ocean's grand, majestic nature remains undisturbed and unchanged, so even though all the senses bring in sensations from nature, the ocean-like heart of the sage knows no disturbance, knows no fear." (Ibid. 70.) Let miseries come in millions of rivers and happiness in hundreds! I am no slave to misery! I am no slave to happiness!

❑

Krishna

This article was recorded by Ida Ansell in shorthand. As, however, Swamiji's speed was too great for her in her early days, dots are put in the articles to indicate the omissions, while the words within square brackets are added by way of linking up the disconnected parts.

(Delivered in California, on April 1, 1900)

Almost the same circumstances which gave birth to Buddhism in India surrounded the rise of Krishna. Not only this, the events of that day we find happening in our own times.

There is a certain ideal. At the same time there must always be a large majority of the human race who cannot come up to the ideal, not even intellectually. ... The strong ones carry it out and many times have no sympathy for the weak. The weak to the strong are only beggars. The strong ones march ahead. ... Of course, we see at once that the highest position to take is to be sympathetic and helpful to those who are weak. But then, in many cases the philosopher bars the way to our being sympathetic. If we go by the theory that the whole of this infinite life has to be determined by the few years' existence here and now, ... then it is very hopeless for us, ... and we have no time to look back upon those who are weak. But if these are not the conditions – if the world is only one of the many schools through which we have to pass, if the eternal life is to be moulded and fashioned and guided by the eternal law, and eternal law, eternal chances await everyone – then we need not be in a hurry. We have time to sympathise, to look around, stretch out a helping hand to the weak and bring them up.

With Buddhism we have two words in Sanskrit: one is translated religion, the other, a sect. It is the most curious fact that the disciples and descendants of Krishna have no name for their religion [although] foreigners call it Hinduism or Brâhmanism. There is one religion, and there are many sects. The moment you give it a name, individualise it and separate it from the rest, it is a sect, no more a religion. A sect [proclaims] its own truth and declares that there is no truth anywhere else. Religion believes that there has been, and still is, one religion in the world. There never were two religions. It is the same religion [presenting] different aspects in different places. The task is to conceive the proper understanding of the goal and scope of humanity.

This was the great work of Krishna: to clear our eyes and make us look with broader vision upon humanity in its march upward and onward. His was the first heart that was large enough to see truth in all, his the first lips that uttered beautiful words for each and all.

This Krishna preceded Buddha by some thousand years. ... A great many people do not believe that he ever existed. Some believe that [the worship of Krishna grew out of] the old sun worship. There seem to be several Krishnas: one was mentioned in the Upanishads, another was king, another a general. All have been lumped into one Krishna. It does not matter much. The fact is, some individual comes who is unique in spirituality. Then all sorts of legends are invented around him. But, all the Bibles and stories which come to be cast upon this one person have to be recast in [the mould of] his character. All the stories of the New Testament have to be modelled upon the accepted life [and] character of Christ. In all of the Indian stories about Buddha the one central note of that whole life is kept up – sacrifice for others. ...

In Krishna we find ... two ideas [stand] supreme in his message: The first is the harmony of different ideas; the second is non-attachment. A man can attain to perfection, the highest goal, sitting on a throne, commanding armies, working out big plans for nations. In fact, Krishna's great sermon was preached on the battlefield.

Krishna saw plainly through the vanity of all the mummeries, mockeries, and ceremonials of the old priests; and yet he saw some good in them.

If you are a strong man, very good! But do not curse others who are not strong enough for you. ... Everyone says, "Woe unto you people! !"

Who says, "Woe unto me that I cannot help you?" The people are doing all right to the best of their ability and means and knowledge. Woe unto me that I cannot lift them to where I am!

So the ceremonials, worship of gods, and myths, are all right, Krishna says. ... Why? Because they all lead to the same goal. Ceremonies, books, and forms— all these are links in the chain. Get hold! That is the one thing. If you are sincere and have really got hold of one link, do not let go; the rest is bound to come. [But people] do not get hold. They spend the time quarrelling and determining what they should get hold of, and do not get hold of anything. ... We are always after truth, but never want to get it. We simply want the pleasure to go about and ask. We have a lot of energy and spend it that way. That is why Krishna says: Get hold of any one of these chains that are stretched out from the common centre. No one step is greater than another. ... Blame no view of religion so far as it is sincere. Hold on to one of these links, and it will pull you to the centre. Your heart itself will teach all the rest. The teacher within will teach all the creeds, all the philosophies. ...

Krishna talks of himself as God, as Christ does. He sees the Deity in himself. And he says, "None can go a day out of my path. All have to come to me. Whosoever wants to worship in whatsoever form, I give him faith in that form, and through that I meet him. ..."(Gita, IV. 12.) His heart is all for the masses.

Independent, Krishna stands out. The very boldness of it frightens us. We depend upon everything – ... upon a few good words, upon circumstances. When the soul wants to depend upon nothing, not even upon life, that is the height of philosophy, the height of manhood. Worship leads to the same goal. Krishna lays great stress upon worship. Worship God!

Various sorts of worship we see in this world. The sick man is very worshipful to God. ... There is the man who loses his fortune; he also prays very much, to get money. The highest worship is that of the man who loves God for God's sake. [The question may be asked :] "Why should there be so much sorrow if there is a God?" The worshipper replies!" ... There is misery in the world; [but] because of that I do not cease to love God. I do not worship Him to take away my [misery]. I love Him because He is love itself." The other [types of worship] are lower-grade; but Krishna has no condemnation for anything. It is better to do something than to stand still. The man who begins to worship God will grow by degrees and begin to love God for love's sake. ...

How to attain purity living this life? Shall we all go to the forest caves? What good would it do? If the mind is not under control, it is no use living in a cave because the same mind will bring all disturbances there. We will find twenty devils in the cave because all the devils are in the mind. If the mind is under control, we can have the cave anywhere, wherever we are.

It is our own mental attitude which makes the world what it is for us. Our thoughts make things beautiful, our thoughts make things ugly. The whole world is in our own minds. Learn to see things in the proper light. First, believe in this world – that there is meaning behind everything. Everything in the world is good, is holy and beautiful. If you see something evil, think that you are not understanding it in the right light. Throw the burden on yourselves! ... Whenever we are tempted to say that the world is going to the dogs, we ought to analyse ourselves, and we shall find that we have lost the faculty of seeing things as they are.

Work day and night! "Behold, I am the Lord of the Universe. I have no duty. Every duty is bondage. But I work for work's sake. If I ceased to work for a minute, [there would be chaos]."(Ibid. III. 22-23.) So do thou work, without any idea of duty. ...

This world is a play. You are His playmates. Go on and work, without any sorrow, without any misery. See His play in the slums, in the saloons! Work to lift people! Not that they are vile or degraded; Krishna does not say that.

Do you know why so little good work is done? My lady goes to the slum. ... She gives a few ducats and says, "My poor men, take that and be happy!"

... Or my fine woman, walking through the street, sees a poor fellow and throws him five cents. Think of the blasphemy of it! Blessed are we that the Lord has given us his teaching in your own Testament. Jesus says, "Inasmuch as ye have done it unto the least of these my brethren, ye have done it unto me." It is blasphemy to think that you can help anyone. First root out this idea of helping, and then go to worship. God's children are your Master's children. [And children are but different forms of the father.] You are His servant. ... Serve the living God! God comes to you in the blind, in the halt, in the poor, in the weak, in the diabolical. What a glorious chance for you to worship! The moment you think you are "helping", you undo the whole thing and degrade yourself. Knowing this, work. "What follows?" you say. You do not get that heartbreak, that awful misery. ... Then work is no more slavery. It becomes a play, and joy itself. ... Work! Be unattached! That is the whole secret. If you get attached, you become miserable. ...

With everything we do in life we identify ourselves. Here is a man who says harsh words to me. I feel anger coming on me. In a few seconds anger and I are one, and then comes misery. Attach yourselves to the Lord and to nothing else, because everything else is unreal. Attachment to the unreal will bring misery. There is only one Existence that is real, only one Life in which there is neither object nor [subject]. ...

But unattached love will not hurt you. Do anything – marry, have children. ... Do anything you like – nothing will hurt you. Do nothing with the idea of "mine". Duty for duty's sake; work for work's sake. What is that to you? You stand aside.

When we come to that non-attachment, then we can understand the marvellous mystery of the universe; how it is intense activity and vibration, and at the same time intensest peace and calm; how it is work every moment and rest every moment. That is the mystery of the universe – the impersonal and personal in one, the infinite and finite in one. Then we shall find the secret. "He who finds in the midst of intense activity the greatest rest, and in the midst of the greatest rest intense activity, he has become a Yogi." (Ibid. IV. 18.) He alone is a real worker, none else. We do a little work and break ourselves. Why? We become attached to that work. If we do not become attached, side by side with it we have infinite rest. ...

How hard it is to arrive at this sort of non-attachment! Therefore Krishna shows us the lower ways and methods. The easiest way for everyone is to do [his or her] work and not take the results. It is our desire that binds us. If we take the results of actions, whether good or evil, we will have to bear them. But if we work not for ourselves, but all for the glory of the Lord, the results will take care of themselves. "To work you have the right, but not to the fruits thereof." (Ibid. II. 47.) The soldier works for no results. He does his duty. If defeat comes, it belongs to the general, not to the soldier. We do our duty for love's sake – love for the general, love for the Lord. ...

If you are strong, take up the Vedanta philosophy and be independent. If you cannot do that, worship God; if not, worship some image. If you lack strength even to do that, do some good works without the idea of gain. Offer everything you have unto the service of the Lord. Fight on! "Leaves and water and one flower – whosoever lays anything on my altar, I receive it with equal delights."(Ibid IX. 26.) If you cannot do anything, not a single good work, then take refuge [in the Lord]. "The Lord resides within the heart of the being, making them turn upon His wheel. Do thou with all thy soul and heart take refuge in Him. ...(Ibid XVIII. 61-62.)

These are some of the general ideas that Krishna preached on this idea of love [in the Gita]. There are [in] other great books, sermons on love – as with Buddha, as with Jesus. ...

A few words about the life of Krishna. There is a great deal of similarity between the lives of Jesus and Krishna. A discussion is going on as to which borrowed of the other. There was the tyrannical king in both places. Both were born in a manger. The parents were bound in both cases. Both were saved by angels. In both cases all the boys born in that year were killed. The childhood is the same. ... Again, in the end, both were killed. Krishna was killed by accident; he took the man who killed him to heaven. Christ was killed, and blessed the robber and took him to heaven.

There are a great many similarities in of the New Testament and the Gita. The human thought goes the same way. ... I will find you the answer in the words of Krishna himself: "Whenever virtue subsides and irreligion prevails, I come down. Again and again I come. Therefore, whenever thou seest a great soul struggling to uplift mankind, know that I am come, and worship. ..."(Ibid. IV. 8; X. 41.)

At the same time, if he comes as Jesus or as Buddha, why is there so much schism? The preachings must be followed! A Hindu devotee would say: It is God himself who became Christ and Krishna and Buddha and all these [great teachers]. A Hindu philosopher would say: These are the great souls; they are already free. And though free, they refuse to accept their liberation while the whole world is suffering. They come again and again, take a human embodiment and help mankind. They know from their childhood what they are and what they come for. ... They do not come through bondage like we do. ... They come out of their own free will, and cannot help having tremendous spiritual power. We cannot resist it. The vast mass of mankind is dragged into the whirlpool of spirituality, and the vibration goes on and on because one of these [great souls] gives a push. So it continues until all mankind is liberated and the play of this planet is finished.

Glory unto the great souls whose lives we have been studying! They are the living gods of the world. They are the persons whom we ought to worship. If He comes to me, I can only recognise Him if He takes a human form. He is everywhere, but do we see Him? We can only see Him if He takes the limitation of man. .... If men and ... animals are manifestations of God, these teachers of mankind are leaders, are Gurus. Therefore, salutations unto you, whose footstool is worshipped by angels! Salutations unto you leaders of the human race! Salutations unto you great teachers! You leaders have our salutations for ever and ever!

❑

Mohammed

This article was recorded by Ida Ansell in shorthand. As, however, Swamiji's speed was too great for her in her early days, dots are put in the articles to indicate the omissions, while the words within square brackets are added by way of linking up the disconnected parts.

(Delivered on March 25, 1900, in the San Francisco Bay Area)

The ancient message of Krishna is one harmonising three – Buddha's, Christ's and Mohammed's. Each of the three started an idea and carried it to its extreme. Krishna antedates all the other prophets. [Yet, we might say,] Krishna takes the old ideas and synthesises them, [although] his is the most ancient message. His message was for the time being submerged by the advance wave of Buddhism. Today it is the message peculiar to India. If you will have it so, this afternoon I will take Mohammed and bring out the particular work of the great Arabian prophet....

Mohammed [as] a young man ... did not [seem to] care much for religion. He was inclined to make money. He was considered a nice young man and very handsome. There was a rich widow. She fell in love with this young man, and they married. When Mohammed had become emperor over the larger part of the world, the Roman and Persian empires were all under his feet, and he had a number of wives. When one day he was asked which wife he liked best, he pointed to his first wife: "Because she believed [in] me first." Women have faith.... Gain independence, gain everything, but do not lose that characteristic of women! ...

Mohammed's heart was sick at the sin, idolatry and mock worship, superstitions and human sacrifices, and so on. The Jews were degraded by the Christians. On the other hand, the Christians were worse degraded than his own countrymen.

We are always in a hurry. [But] if any great work is to be done, there must be great preparation. ... After much praying, day and night, Mohammed began to have dreams and visions. Gabriel appeared to him in a dream and told him that he was the messenger of truth. He told him that the message of Jesus, of Moses, and all the prophets would be lost and asked him to go and preach. Seeing the Christians preaching politics in the name of Jesus, seeing the Persians preaching dualism, Mohammed said: "Our God is one God. He is the Lord of all that exists. There is no comparison between Him and any other."

God is God. There is no philosophy, no complicated code of ethics. "Our God is one without a second, and Mohammed is the Prophet." ... Mohammed began to preach it in the streets of Mecca. ... They began to persecute him, and he fled into the city of [Medina]. He began to fight, and the whole race became united. [Mohammedanism] deluged the world in the name of the Lord. The tremendous conquering power! ...

You ... people have very hard ideas and are so superstitious and prejudiced! These messengers must have come from God, else how could they have been so great? You look at every defect. Each one of us has his defects. Who hasn't? I can point out many defects in the Jews. The wicked are always looking for defects. ... Flies come and seek for the [ulcer], and bees come only for the honey in the flower. Do not follow the way of the fly but that of the bee....

Mohammed married quite a number of wives afterwards. Great men may marry two hundred wives each. "Giants" like you, I would not allow to marry one wife. The characters of the great souls are mysterious, their methods past our finding out. We must not judge them. Christ may judge Mohammed. Who are you and I? Little babies. What do we understand of these great souls? ...

[Mohammedanism] came as a message for the masses. ... The first message was equality. ... There is one religion – love. No more question of race, colour, [or] anything else. Join it! That practical quality carried the day. ... The great message was perfectly simple. Believe in one God, the creator of heaven and earth. All was created out of nothing by Him. Ask no questions. ...

Their temples are like Protestant churches. ... no music, no paintings, no pictures. A pulpit in the corner; on that lies the Koran. The people all stand in line. No priest, no person, no bishop. ... The man who prays must stand at the side of the audience. Some parts are beautiful. ...

These old people were all messengers of God. I fall down and worship them; I take the dust of their feet. But they are dead! ... And we are alive. We must go ahead! ... Religion is not an imitation of Jesus or Mohammed. Even if an imitation is good, it is never genuine. Be not an imitation of Jesus, but be Jesus,

You are quite as great as Jesus, Buddha, or anybody else. If we are not ... we must struggle and be. I would not be exactly like Jesus. It is unnecessary that I should be born a Jew. ...

The greatest religion is to be true to your own nature. Have faith in yourselves! If you do not exist, how can God exist, or anybody else? Wherever you are, it is this mind that perceives even the Infinite. I see God, therefore He exists. If I cannot think of God, He does not exist [for me]. This is the grand march of our human progress.

These [great souls] are signposts on the way. That is all they are. They say, "Onward, brothers!"

We cling to them; we never want to move. We do not want to think; we want others to think for us. The messengers fulfil their mission. They ask to be up and doing. A hundred years later we cling to the message and go to sleep.

Talking about faith and belief and doctrine is easy, but it is so difficult to build character and to stem the tide of the senses. We succumb. We become hypocrites. ...

[Religion] is not a doctrine, [not] a rule. It is a process. That is all. [Doctrines and rules] are all for exercise. By that exercise we get strong and at last break the bonds and become free. Doctrine is of no use except for gymnastics. ... Through exercise the soul becomes perfect. That exercise is stopped when you say, "I believe." ...

"Whenever virtue subsides and immorality abounds, I take human form. In every age I come for the salvation of the good, for the destruction of the wicked, for the establishment of spirituality." (Gita, IV. 7-8.)

[Such] are the great messengers of light. They are our great teachers, our elder brothers. But we must go our own way!

❑

One Existence Appearing as Many

(Delivered in New York, 1896)

Vairâgya or renunciation is the turning point in all the various Yogas. The Karmi (worker) renounces the fruits of his work. The Bhakta (devotee) renounces all little loves for the almighty and omnipresent love. The Yogi renounces his experiences, because his philosophy is that the whole Nature, although it is for the experience of the soul, at last brings him to know that he is not in Nature, but eternally separate from Nature. The Jnâni (philosopher) renounces everything, because his philosophy is that Nature never existed, neither in the past, nor present, nor will It in the future. The question of utility cannot be asked in these higher themes. It is very absurd to ask it; and even if it be asked, after a proper analysis, what do we find in this question of utility? The ideal of happiness, that which brings man more happiness, is of greater utility to him than these higher things which do not improve his material conditions or bring him such great happiness. All the sciences are for this one end, to bring happiness to humanity; and that which brings the larger amount of happiness, man takes and gives up that which brings a lesser amount of happiness. We have seen how happiness is either in the body, or in the mind, or in the Âtman. With animals, and in the lowest human beings who are very much like animals, happiness is all in the body. No man can eat with the same pleasure as a famished dog or a wolf; so in the dog and the wolf the happiness is entirely in the body. In men we find a higher plane of happiness, that of thought; and in the Jnani there is the highest plane of happiness in the Self, the Atman. So to the philosopher this knowledge of the Self is of the highest utility, because it gives him the highest happiness possible. Sense-gratifications or physical things cannot be of the highest utility to him, because he does not find in them the same pleasure that he finds in knowledge itself; and after all, knowledge is the one goal and is really the highest happiness that we know. All who work in ignorance are, as it were, the draught animals of the Devas. The word Deva is here used in the sense of a wise man. All the people that work and toil and labour like machines do not really enjoy life, but it is the wise man who enjoys. A rich man buys a picture at a cost of a hundred thousand dollars perhaps, but it is the man who understands art that enjoys it; and if the rich man is without knowledge of art, it is useless to him, he is only the owner. All over the world, it is the wise man who enjoys the happiness of the world. The ignorant man never enjoys; he has to work for others unconsciously.

Thus far we have seen the theories of these Advaitist philosophers, how there is but one Atman; there cannot be two. We have seen how in the whole of this universe there is but One Existence; and that One Existence when seen through the senses is called the world, the world of matter. When It is seen through the mind, It is called the world of thoughts and ideas; and when It is seen as it is, then It is the One Infinite Being. You must bear this in mind; it is not that there is a soul in man, although I had to take that for granted in order to explain it at first, but that there is only One Existence, and that one the Atman, the Self; and when this is perceived through the senses, through sense-imageries, It is called the body. When It is perceived through thought, It is called the mind. When It is perceived in Its own nature, It is the Atman, the One Only Existence. So it is not that there are three things in one, the body and the mind and the Self, although that was a convenient way of putting it in the course of explanation; but all is that Atman, and that one Being is sometimes called the body, sometimes the mind, and sometimes the Self, according to different vision. There is but one Being which the ignorant call the world. When a man goes higher in knowledge, he calls the very same Being the world of thought. Again, when knowledge itself comes, all illusions vanish, and man finds it is all nothing but Atman. I am that One Existence. This is the last conclusion. There are neither three nor two in the universe; it is all One. That One, under the illusion of Maya, is seen as many, just as a rope is seen as a snake. It is the very rope that is seen as a snake. There are not two things there, a rope separate and a snake separate. No man sees these two things there at the same time. Dualism and non-dualism are very good philosophic terms, but in perfect perception we never perceive the real and the false at the same time. We are all born monists, we cannot help it. We always perceive the one. When we perceive the rope, we do not perceive the snake at all; and when we see the snake, we do not see the rope at all – it has vanished. When you see illusion, you do not see reality. Suppose you see one of your friends coming at a distance in the street; you know him very well, but through the haze and mist that is before you, you think it is another man. When you see your friend as another man, you do not see your friend at all, he has vanished. You are perceiving only one. Suppose your friend is Mr. A; but when you perceive Mr. A as Mr. B. you do not see Mr. A at all. In each case you perceive only one. When you see yourself as a body, you are body and nothing else; and that is the perception of the vast majority of mankind. They may talk of soul and mind, and all these things, but what they perceive is the physical form, the touch, taste, vision, and so on. Again, with certain men in certain states of consciousness, they perceive themselves as thought. You know, of course, the story told of Sir Humphrey Davy, who has making experiments before his class with laughing-gas, and suddenly one of the tubes broke, and the gas escaping, he breathed it in. For some moments he remained like a statue. Afterwards he told his class that when he was in that state, he actually perceived that the whole world is made up of ideas. The gas, for a time, made him forget the consciousness of the body, and that very thing which he was seeing as the body, he began to perceive as ideas. When the consciousness rises still higher, when this little puny consciousness is gone for ever, that which is the Reality behind shines, and we see it as the One Existence-Knowledge-Bliss, the one Atman, the Universal. "One that is only Knowledge itself, One that is Bliss itself, beyond all compare, beyond all limit, ever free, never bound, infinite as the sky, unchangeable as the sky. Such a One will manifest Himself in your heart in meditation."

How does the Advaitist theory explain these various phases of heaven and hells and these various ideas we find in all religions? When a man dies, it is said that he goes to heaven or hell, goes here or there, or that when a man dies he is born again in another body either in heaven or in another world or somewhere. These are all hallucinations. Really speaking nobody is ever born or dies. There is neither heaven nor hell nor this world; all three never really existed. Tell a child a lot of ghost stories, add let him go out into the street in the evening. There is a little stump of a tree. What does the child see? A ghost, with hands stretched out, ready to grab him. Suppose a man comes from the corner of the street, wanting to meet his sweetheart; he sees that stump of the tree as the girl. A policeman coming from the street corner sees the stump as a thief. The thief sees it as a policeman. It is the same stump of a tree that was seen in various ways. The stump is the reality, and the visions of the stump are the projections of the various minds. There is one Being, this Self; It neither comes nor goes. When a man is ignorant, he wants to go to heaven or some place, and all his life he has been thinking and thinking of this; and when this earth dream vanishes, he sees this world as a heaven with Devas and angels flying about, and all such things. If a man all his life desires to meet his forefathers, he gets them all from Adam downwards, because he creates them. If a man is still more ignorant and has always been frightened by fanatics with ideas of hell, with all sorts of punishments, when he dies, he will see this very world as hell. All that is meant by dying or being born is simply changes in the plane of vision. Neither do you move, nor does that move upon which you project your vision. You are the permanent, the unchangeable. How can you come and go? It is impossible; you are omnipresent. The sky never moves, but the clouds move over the surface of the sky, and we may think that the sky itself moves, just as when you are in a railway train, you think the land is moving. It is not so, but it is the train which is moving. You are where you are; these dreams, these various clouds move. One dream follows another without connection. There is no such thing as law or connection in this world, but we are thinking that there is a great deal of connection. All of you have probably read Alice in Wonderland. It is the most wonderful book for children that has been written in this century When I read it, I was delighted; it was always in my head to write that sort of a book for children. What pleased me most in it was what you think most incongruous, that there is no connection there. One idea comes and jumps into another, without any connection. When you were children, you thought that the most wonderful connection. So this man brought back his thoughts of childhood, which were perfectly connected to him as a child, and composed this book for children. And all these books which men write, trying to make children swallow their own ideas as men, are nonsense. We too are grown-up children, that is all. The world is the same unconnected thing – Alice in Wonderland – with no connection whatever. When we see things happen a number of times in a certain sequence, we call it cause and effect, and say that the thing will happen again. When this dream changes, another dream will seem quite as connected as this. When we dream, the things we see all seem to be connected; during the dream we never think they are incongruous; it is only when we wake that we see the want of connection. When we wake from this dream of the world and compare it with the Reality, it will be found all incongruous nonsense, a mass of incongruity passing before us, we do not know whence or whither, but we know it will end; and this is called Maya, and is like masses of fleeting fleecy clouds. They represent all this changing existence, and the sun itself, the unchanging, is you. When you look at that unchanging Existence from the outside, you call it God; and when you look at it from the inside, you call it yourself. It is but one. There is no God separate from you, no God higher than you, the real "you". All the gods are little beings to you, all the ideas of God and Father in heaven are but your own reflection. God Himself is your image. "God created man after His own image." That is wrong. Man creates God after his own image. That is right. Throughout the universe we are creating gods after our own image. We create the god and fall down at his feet and worship him; and when this dream comes, we love it!

This is a good point to understand – that the sum and substance of this lecture is that there is but One Existence, and that One-Existence seen through different constitutions appears either as the earth, or heaven, or hell, or gods, or ghosts, or men, or demons, or world, or all these things. But among these many, "He who sees that One in this ocean of death, he who sees that One Life in this floating universe, who realises that One who never changes, unto him belongs eternal peace; unto none else, unto none else." This One existence has to be realised. How, is the next question. How is it to be realised? How is this dream to be broken, how shall we wake up from this dream that we are little men and women, and all such things? We are the Infinite Being of the universe and have become materialised into these little beings, men and women, depending upon the sweet word of one man, or the angry word of another, and so forth. What a terrible dependence, what a terrible slavery! I who am beyond all pleasure and pain, whose reflection is the whole universe, little bits of whose life are the suns and moons and stars – I am held down as a terrible slave! If you pinch my body, I feel pain. If one says a kind word, I begin to rejoice. See my condition – slave of the body, slave of the mind, slave of the world, slave of a good word, slave of a bad word, slave of passion, slave of happiness, slave of life, slave of death, slave of everything! This slavery has to be broken. How? "This Atman has first to be heard, then reasoned upon, and then meditated upon." This is the method of the Advaita Jnâni. The truth has to be heard, then reflected upon, and then to be constantly asserted. Think always, "I am Brahman". Every other thought must be cast aside as weakening. Cast aside every thought that says that you are men or women. Let body go, and mind go, and gods go, and ghosts go. Let everything go but that One Existence. "Where one hears another, where one sees another, that is small; where one does not hear another, where one does not see another, that is Infinite." That is the highest when the subject and the object become one. When I am the listener and I am the speaker, when I am the teacher and I am the taught, when I am the creator and I am the created – then alone fear ceases; there is not another to make us afraid. There is nothing but myself, what can frighten me? This is to be heard day after day. Get rid of all other thoughts. Everything else must be thrown aside, and this is to be repeated continually, poured through the ears until it reaches the heart, until every nerve and muscle, every drop of blood tingles with the idea that I am He, I am He. Even at the gate of death say, "I am He". There was a man in India, a Sannyâsin, who used to repeat "Shivoham" – "I am Bliss Eternal"; and a tiger jumped on him one day and dragged him away and killed him; but so long as he was living, the sound came, "Shivoham, Shivoham". Even at the gate of death, in the greatest danger, in the thick of the battlefield, at the bottom of the ocean, on the tops of the highest mountains, in the thickest of the forest, tell yourself, "I am He, I am He". Day and night say, "I am He". It is the greatest strength; it is religion. "The weak will never reach the Atman." Never say, "O Lord, I am a miserable sinner." Who will help you? You are the help of the universe. What in this universe can help you? Where is the man, or the god, or the demon to help you? What can prevail over you? You are the God of the universe; where can you seek for help? Never help came from anywhere but from yourself. In your ignorance, every prayer that you made and that was answered, you thought was answered by some Being, but you answered the prayer yourself unknowingly. The help came from yourself, and you fondly imagined that some one was sending help to you. There is no help for you outside of yourself; you are the creator of the universe. Like the silkworm you have built a cocoon around yourself. Who will save you? Burst your own cocoon and come out as the beautiful butterfly, as the free soul. Then alone you will see Truth. Ever tell yourself, "I am He." These are words that will burn up the dross that is in the mind, words that will bring out the tremendous energy which is within you already, the infinite power which is sleeping in your heart. This is to be brought out by constantly hearing the truth and nothing else. Wherever there is thought of weakness, approach not the place. Avoid all weakness if you want to be a Jnani.

Before you begin to practice, clear your mind of all doubts. Fight and reason and argue; and when you have established it in your mind that this and this alone can be the truth and nothing else, do not argue any more; close your mouth. Hear not argumentation, neither argue yourself. What is the use of any more arguments? You have satisfied yourself, you have decided the question. What remains? The truth has now to be realised, therefore why waste valuable time in vain arguments? The truth has now to be meditated upon, and every idea that strengthens you must be taken up and every thought that weakens you must be rejected. The Bhakta meditates upon forms and images and all such things and upon God. This is the natural process, but a slower one. The Yogi meditates upon various centres in his body and manipulates powers in his mind. The Jnani says, the mind does not exist, neither the body. This idea of the body and of the mind must go, must be driven off; therefore it is foolish to think of them. It would be like trying to cure one ailment by bringing in another. His meditation therefore is the most difficult one, the negative; he denies everything, and what is left is the Self. This is the most analytical way. The Jnani wants to tear away the universe from the Self by the sheer force of analysis. It is very easy to say, "I am a Jnani", but very hard to be really one. "The way is long", it is, as it were, walking on the sharp edge of a razor; yet despair not. "Awake, arise, and stop not until the goal is reached", say the Vedas.

So what is the meditation of the Jnani? He wants to rise above every idea of body or mind, to drive away the idea that he is the body. For instance, when I say, "I Swami", immediately the idea of the body comes. What must I do then? I must give the mind a hard blow and say, "No, I am not the body, I am the Self." Who cares if disease comes or death in the most horrible form? I am not the body. Why make the body nice? To enjoy the illusion once more? To continue the slavery? Let it go, I am not the body. That is the way of the Jnani. The Bhakta says, "The Lord has given me this body that I may safely cross the ocean of life, and I must cherish it until the journey is accomplished." The Yogi says, "I must be careful of the body, so that I may go on steadily and finally attain liberation." The Jnani feels that he cannot wait, he must reach the goal this very moment. He says, "I am free through eternity, I am never bound; I am the God of the universe through all eternity. Who shall make me perfect? I am perfect already." When a man is perfect, he sees perfection in others. When he sees imperfection, it is his own mind projecting itself. How can he see imperfection if he has not got it in himself? So the Jnani does not care for perfection or imperfection. None exists for him. As soon as he is free, he does not see good and evil. Who sees evil and good? He who has it in himself. Who sees the body? He who thinks he is the body. The moment you get rid of the idea that you are the body, you do not see the world at all; it vanishes for ever. The Jnani seeks to tear himself away from this bondage of matter by the force of intellectual conviction. This is the negative way – the "Neti, Neti" – "Not this, not this."

❑

The Free Soul

(Delivered in New York, 1896)

The analysis of the Sânkhyas stops with the duality of existence – Nature and souls. There are an infinite number of souls, which, being simple, cannot die, and must therefore be separate from Nature. Nature in itself changes and manifests all these phenomena; and the soul, according to the Sankhyas, is inactive. It is a simple by itself, and Nature works out all these phenomena for the liberation of the soul; and liberation consists in the soul discriminating that it is not Nature. At the same time we have seen that the Sankhyas were bound to admit that every soul was omnipresent. Being a simple, the soul cannot be limited, because all limitation comes either through time, space, or causation. The soul being entirely beyond these cannot have any limitation. To have limitation one must be in space, which means the body; and that which is body must be in Nature. If the soul had form, it would be identified with Nature; therefore the soul is formless, and that which is formless cannot be said to exist here, there, or anywhere. It must be omnipresent. Beyond this the Sankhya philosophy does not go.

The first argument of the Vedantists against this is that this analysis is not a perfect one. If their Nature be absolute and the soul be also absolute, there will be two absolutes, and all the arguments that apply in the case of the soul to show that it is omnipresent will apply in the case of Nature, and Nature too will be beyond all time, space, and causation, and as the result there will be no change or manifestation. Then will come the difficulty of having two absolutes, which is impossible. What is the solution of the Vedantist? His solution is that, just as the Sankhyas say, it requires some sentient Being as the motive power behind, which makes the mind think and Nature work, because Nature in all its modifications, from gross matter up to Mahat (Intelligence), is simply insentient. Now, says the Vedantist, this sentient Being which is behind the whole universe is what we call God, and consequently this universe is not different from Him. It is He Himself who has become this universe. He not only is the instrumental cause of this universe, but also the material cause. Cause is never different from effect, the effect is but the cause reproduced in another form. We see that every day. So this Being is the cause of Nature. All the forms and phases of Vedanta, either dualistic, or qualified-monistic, or monistic, first take this position that God is not only the instrumental, but also the material cause of this universe, that everything which exists is He. The second step in Vedanta is that these souls are also a part of God, one spark of that Infinite Fire. "As from a mass of fire millions of small particles fly, even so from this Ancient One have come all these souls." So far so good, but it does not yet satisfy. What is meant by a part of the Infinite? The Infinite is indivisible; there cannot be parts of the Infinite. The Absolute cannot be divided. What is meant, therefore, by saying that all these sparks are from Him? The Advaitist, the non-dualistic Vedantist, solves the problem by maintaining that there is really no part; that each soul is really not a part of the Infinite, but actually is the Infinite Brahman. Then how can there be so many? The sun reflected from millions of globules of water appears to be millions of suns, and in each globule is a miniature picture of the sun-form; so all these souls are but reflections and not real. They are not the real "I" which is the God of this universe, the one undivided Being of the universe. And all these little different beings, men and animals etc. are but reflections, and not real. They are simply illusory reflections upon Nature. There is but one Infinite Being in the universe, and that Being appears as you and as I; but this appearance of divisions is after all a delusion. He has not been divided, but only appears to be divided. This apparent division is caused by looking at Him through the network of time, space, and causation. When I look at God through the network of time, space, and causation, I see Him as the material world. When I look at Him from a little higher plane, yet through the same network, I see Him as an animal, a little higher as a man, a little higher as a god, but yet He is the One Infinite Being of the universe, and that Being we are. I am That, and you are That. Not parts of It, but the whole of It. "It is the Eternal Knower standing behind the whole phenomena; He Himself is the phenomena." He is both the subject and the object, He is the "I" and the "You". How is this? "How to know the Knower? The Knower cannot know Himself; I see everything but cannot see myself. The Self, the Knower, the Lord of all, the Real Being, is the cause of all the vision that is in the universe, but it is impossible for Him to see Himself or know Himself, excepting through reflection. You cannot see your own face except in a mirror, and so the Self cannot see Its own nature until

It is reflected, and this whole universe therefore is the Self trying to realise Itself. This reflection is thrown back first from the protoplasm, then from plants and animals, and so on and on from better and better reflectors, until the best reflector, the perfect man, is reached – just as a man who, wanting to see his face, looks first in a little pool of muddy water, and sees just an outline; then he comes to clear water, and sees a better image; then to a piece of shining metal, and sees a still better image; and at last to a looking-glass, and sees himself reflected as he is. Therefore the perfect man is the highest reflection of that Being who is both subject and object. You now find why man instinctively worships everything, and how perfect men are instinctively worshipped as God in every country. You may talk as you like, but it is they who are bound to be worshipped. That is why men worship Incarnations, such as Christ or Buddha. They are the most perfect manifestations of the eternal Self. They are much higher than all the conceptions of God that you or I can make. A perfect man is much higher than such conceptions. In him the circle becomes complete; the subject and the object become one. In him all delusions go away and in their place comes the realisation that he has always been that perfect Being. How came this bondage then? How was it possible for this perfect Being to degenerate into the imperfect? How was it possible that the free became bound? The Advaitist says, he was never bound, but was always free. Various clouds of various colours come before the sky. They remain there a minute and then pass away. It is the same eternal blue sky stretching there for ever. The sky never changes: it is the cloud that is changing. So you are always perfect, eternally perfect. Nothing ever changes your nature, or ever will. All these ideas that I am imperfect, I am a man, or a woman, or a sinner, or I am the mind, I have thought, I will think – all are hallucinations; you never think, you never had a body; you never were imperfect. You are the blessed Lord of this universe, the one Almighty ruler of everything that is and ever will be, the one mighty ruler of these suns and stars and moons and earths and planets and all the little bits of our universe. It is through you that the sun shines and the stars shed their lustre, and the earth becomes beautiful. It is through your blessedness that they all love and are attracted to each other. You are in all, and you are all. Whom to avoid, and whom to take? You are the all in all. When this knowledge comes delusion immediately vanishes.

I was once travelling in the desert in India. I travelled for over a month and always found the most beautiful landscapes before me, beautiful lakes and all that. One day I was very thirsty and I wanted to have a drink at one of these lakes; but when I approached that lake it vanished. Immediately with a blow came into my brain the idea that this was a mirage about which I had read all my life; and then I remembered and smiled at my folly, that for the last month all the beautiful landscapes and lakes I had been seeing were this mirage, but I could not distinguish them then. The next morning I again began my march; there was the lake and the landscape, but with it immediately came the idea, "This is a mirage." Once known it had lost its power of illusion. So this illusion of the universe will break one day. The whole of this will vanish, melt away. This is realization. Philosophy is no joke or talk. It has to be realised; this body will vanish, this earth and everything will vanish, this idea that I am the body or the mind will for some time vanish, or if the Karma is ended it will disappear, never to come back; but if one part of the Karma remains, then as a potter's wheel, after the potter has finished the pot, will sometimes go on from the past momentum, so this body, when the delusion has vanished altogether, will go on for some time. Again this world will come, men and women and animals will come, just as the mirage came the next day, but not with the same force; along with it will come the idea that I know its nature now, and it will cause no bondage, no more pain, nor grief, nor misery. Whenever anything miserable will come, the mind will be able to say, "I know you as hallucination." When a man has reached that state, he is called Jivanmukta, living-free", free even while living. The aim and end in this life for the

Jnâna-Yogi is to become this Jivanmukta, "living-free". He is Jivanmukta who can live in this world without being attached. He is like the lotus leaves in water, which are never wetted by the water. He is the highest of human beings, nay, the highest of all beings, for he has realised his identity with the Absolute, he has realised that he is one with God. So long as you think you have the least difference from God, fear will seize you, but when you have known that you are He, that there is no difference, entirely no difference, that you are He, all of Him, and the whole of Him, all fear ceases. "There, who sees whom? Who worships whom? Who talks to whom? Who hears whom? Where one sees another, where one talks to another, where one hears another, that is little. Where none sees none, where none speaks to none, that is the highest, that is the great, that is the Brahman." Being That, you are always That. What will become of the world then? What good shall we do to the world? Such questions do not arise "What becomes of my gingerbread if I become old?" says the baby! "What becomes of my marbles if I grow? So I will not grow," says the boy! "What will become of my dolls if I grow old?" says the little child! It is the same question in connection with this world, it has no existence in the past, present, or future. If we have known the Âtman as It is, if we have known that there is nothing else but this Atman, that everything else is but a dream, with no existence in reality, then this world with its poverties, its miseries, its wickedness, and its goodness will cease to disturb us. If they do not exist, for whom and for what shall we take trouble? This is what the Jnana-Yogis teach. Therefore, dare to be free, dare to go as far as your thought leads, and dare to carry that out in your life. It is very hard to come to Jnâna. It is for the bravest and most daring, who dare to smash all idols, not only intellectual, but in the senses. This body is not I; it must go. All sorts of curious things may come out of this. A man stands up and says, "I am not the body, therefore my headache must be cured"; but where is the headache if not in his body? Let a thousand headaches and a thousand bodies come and go. What is that to me? I have neither birth nor death; father or mother I never had; friends and foes I have none, because they are all I. I am my own friend, and I am my own enemy. I am Existence-Knowledge-Bliss Absolute. I am He, I am He. If in a thousand bodies I am suffering from fever and other ills, in millions of bodies I am healthy. If in a thousand bodies I am starving, in other thousand bodies I am feasting. If in thousands of bodies I am suffering misery, in thousands of bodies I am happy. Who shall blame whom, who praise whom? Whom to seek, whom to avoid? I seek none, nor avoid any, for I am all the universe. I praise myself, I blame myself, I suffer for myself, I am happy at my own will, I am free. This is the Jnâni, the brave and daring. Let the whole universe tumble down; he smiles and says it never existed, it was all a hallucination. He sees the universe tumble down. Where was it! Where has it gone!

Before going into the practical part, we will take up one more intellectual question. So far the logic is tremendously rigorous. If man reasons, there is no place for him to stand until he comes to this, that there is but One Existence, that everything else is nothing. There is no other way left for rational mankind but to take this view. But how is it that what is infinite, ever perfect, ever blessed, Existence-Knowledge-Bliss Absolute, has come under these delusions? It is the same question that has been asked all the world over. In the vulgar form the question becomes, "How did sin come into this world?" This is the most vulgar and sensuous form of the question, and the other is the most philosophic form, but the answer is the same. The same question has been asked in various grades and fashions, but in its lower forms it finds no solution, because the stories of apples and serpents and women do not give the explanation. In that state, the question is childish, and so is the answer. But the question has assumed very high proportions now: "How did this illusion come?" And the answer is as fine. The answer is that we cannot expect any answer to an impossible question. The very question is impossible in terms. You have no right to ask that question. Why? What is perfection?

That which is beyond time, space, and causation – that is perfect. Then you ask how the perfect became imperfect. In logical language the question may be put in this form: "How did that which is beyond causation become caused?" You contradict yourself. You first admit it is beyond causation, and then ask what causes it. This question can only be asked within the limits of causation. As far as time and space and causation extend, so far can this question be asked. But beyond that it will be nonsense to ask it, because the question is illogical. Within time, space, and causation it can never be answered, and what answer may lie beyond these limits can only be known when we have transcended them; therefore the wise will let this question rest. When a man is ill, he devotes himself to curing his disease without insisting that he must first learn how he came to have it.

There is another form of this question, a little lower, but more practical and illustrative: What produced this delusion? Can any reality produce delusion? Certainly not. We see that one delusion produces another, and so on. It is delusion always that produces delusion. It is disease that produces disease, and not health that produces disease. The wave is the same thing as the water, the effect is the cause in another form. The effect is delusion, and therefore the cause must be delusion. What produced this delusion? Another delusion. And so on without beginning. The only question that remains for you to ask is: Does not this break your monism, because you get two existences in the universe, one yourself and the other the delusion? The answer is: Delusion cannot be called an existence. Thousands of dreams come into your life, but do not form any part of your life. Dreams come and go; they have no existence. To call delusion existence will be sophistry. Therefore there is only one individual existence in the universe, ever free, and ever blessed; and that is what you are. This is the last conclusion reached by the Advaitists.

It may then be asked: What becomes of all these various forms of worship? They will remain; they are simply groping in the dark for light, and through this groping light will come. We have just seen that the Self cannot see Itself. Our knowledge is within the network of Mâyâ (unreality), and beyond that is freedom. Within the network there is slavery, it is all under law; beyond that there is no law. So far as the universe is concerned, existence is ruled by law, and beyond that is freedom. As long as you are in the network of time, space, and causation, to say you are free is nonsense, because in that network all is under rigorous law, sequence, and consequence. Every thought that you think is caused, every feeling has been caused; to say that the will is free is sheer nonsense. It is only when the infinite existence comes, as it were, into this network of Maya that it takes the form of will. Will is a portion of that being, caught in the network of Maya, and therefore "free will" is a misnomer. It means nothing – sheer nonsense. So is all this talk about freedom. There is no freedom in Maya.

Every one is as much bound in thought, word, deed, and mind, as a piece of stone or this table. That I talk to you now is as rigorous in causation as that you listen to me. There is no freedom until you go beyond Maya. That is the real freedom of the soul. Men, however sharp and intellectual, however clearly they see the force of the logic that nothing here can be free, are all compelled to think they are free; they cannot help it. No work can go on until we begin to say we are free. It means that the freedom we talk about is the glimpse of the blue sky through the clouds and that the real freedom – the blue sky itself— is behind. True freedom cannot exist in the midst of this delusion, this hallucination, this nonsense of the world, this universe of the senses, body, and mind. All these dreams, without beginning or end, uncontrolled and uncontrollable, ill-adjusted, broken, inharmonious, form our idea of this universe. In a dream, when you see a giant with twenty heads chasing you, and you are flying from him, you do not think it is inharmonious; you think it is proper and right. So is this law. All that you call law is simply chance without meaning. In this dream state you call it law. Within Maya, so far as this law of time, space and causation exists, there is no freedom; and all these various forms of worship are within this Maya. The idea of God and the ideas of brute and of man are within this Maya, and as such are equally hallucinations; all of them are dreams. But you must take care not to argue like some extraordinary men of whom we hear at the present time. They say the idea of God is a delusion, but the idea of this world is true. Both ideas stand or fall by the same logic. He alone has the right to be an atheist who denies this world, as well as the other. The same argument is for both. The same mass of delusion extends from God to the lowest animal, from a blade of grass to the Creator. They stand or fall by the same logic. The same person who sees falsity in the idea of God ought also to see it in the idea of his own body or his own mind. When God vanishes, then also vanish the body and mind; and when both vanish, that which is the Real Existence remains for ever. "There the eyes cannot go, nor the speech, nor the mind. We cannot see it, neither know it." And we now understand that so far as speech and thought and knowledge and intellect go, it is all within this Maya within bondage. Beyond that is Reality. There neither thought, nor mind, nor speech, can reach.

So far it is intellectually all right, but then comes the practice. The real work is in the practice. Are any practices necessary to realise this Oneness? Most decidedly. It is not that you become this Brahman. You are already that. It is not that you are going to become God or perfect; you are already perfect; and whenever you think you are not, it is a delusion. This delusion which says that you are Mr. So-and-so or Mrs. So-and-so can be got rid of by another delusion, and that is practice. Fire will eat fire, and you can use one delusion to conquer another delusion. One cloud will come and brush away another cloud, and then both will go away. What are these practices then? We must always bear in mind that we are not going to be free, but are free already. Every idea that we are bound is a delusion. Every idea that we are happy or unhappy is a tremendous delusion; and another delusion will come – that we have got to work and worship and struggle to be free – and this will chase out the first delusion, and then both will stop.

The fox is considered very unholy by the Mohammedans and by the Hindus. Also, if a dog touches any bit of food, it has to be thrown out, it cannot be eaten by any man. In a certain Mohammedan house a fox entered and took a little bit of food from the table, ate it up, and fled. The man was a poor man, and had prepared a very nice feast for himself, and that feast was made unholy, and he could not eat it. So he went to a Mulla, a priest, and said, "This has happened to me; a fox came and took a mouthful out of my meal. What can be done? I had prepared a feast and wanted so much to eat it, and now comes this fox and destroys the whole affair."

The Mulla thought for a minute and then found only one solution and said, "The only way for you is to get a dog and make him eat a bit out of the same plate, because dogs and foxes are eternally quarrelling. The food that was left by the fox will go into your stomach, and that left by the dog will go there too, and both will be purified." We are very much in the same predicament. This is a hallucination that we are imperfect; and we take up another, that we have to practice to become perfect. Then one will chase the other, as we can use one thorn to extract another and then throw both away. There are people for whom it is sufficient knowledge to hear, "Thou art That". With a flash this universe goes away and the real nature shines, but others have to struggle hard to get rid of this idea of bondage.

The first question is: Who are fit to become Jnana-Yogis? Those who are equipped with these requisites: First, renunciation of all fruits of work and of all enjoyments in this life or another life. If you are the creator of this universe, whatever you desire you will have, because you will create it for yourself. It is only a question of time. Some get it immediately; with others the past Samskâras (impressions) stand in the way of getting their desires. We give the first place to desires for enjoyment, either in this or another life. Deny that there is any life at all; because life is only another name for death. Deny that you are a living being. Who cares for life? Life is one of these hallucinations, and death is its counterpart. Joy is one part of these hallucinations, and misery the other part, and so on. What have you to do with life or death ? These are all creations of the mind. This is called giving up desires of enjoyment either in this life or another.

Then comes controlling the mind, calming it so that it will not break into waves and have all sorts of desires, holding the mind steady, not allowing it to get into waves from external or internal causes, controlling the mind perfectly, just by the power of will. The Jnana-Yogi does not take any one of these physical helps or mental helps: simply philosophic reasoning, knowledge, and his own will, these are the instrumentalities he believes in. Next comes Titikshâ, forbearance, bearing all miseries without murmuring, without complaining. When an injury comes, do not mind it. If a tiger comes, stand there. Who flies? There are men who practice Titiksha, and succeed in it. There are men who sleep on the banks of the Ganga in the midsummer sun of India, and in winter float in the waters of the Ganga for a whole day; they do not care. Men sit in the snow of the Himalayas, and do not care to wear any garment. What is heat? What is cold? Let things come and go, what is that to me, I am not the body. It is hard to believe this in these Western countries, but it is better to know that it is done. Just as your people are brave to jump at the mouth of a cannon, or into the midst of the battlefield, so our people are brave to think and act out their philosophy. They give up their lives for it. "I am Existence-Knowledge-Bliss Absolute; I am He, I am He." Just as the Western ideal is to keep up luxury in practical life, so ours is to keep up the highest form of spirituality, to demonstrate that religion is riot merely frothy words, but can be carried out, every bit of it, in this life. This is Titiksha, to bear everything, not to complain of anything. I myself have seen men who say, "I am the soul; what is the universe to me? Neither pleasure nor pain, nor virtue nor vice, nor heat nor cold is anything to me." That is Titiksha; not running after the enjoyments of the body. What is religion? To pray, "Give me this and that"? Foolish ideas of religion! Those who believe them have no true idea of God and soul. My Master used to say, "The vulture rise higher and higher until he becomes a speck, but his eye is always on the piece of rotten carrion on the earth." After all, what is the result of your ideas of religion? To cleanse the streets and have more bread and clothes? Who cares for bread and clothes? Millions come and go every minute. Who cares? Why care for the joys and vicissitudes of this little world? Go beyond that if you dare; go beyond law, let the whole universe vanish, and stand alone. "I am Existence-Absolute, Knowledge-Absolute, Bliss-Absolute; I am He, I am He."

❑

Unity, The Goal of Religion

(Delivered in New York, 1896)

This universe of ours, the universe of the senses, the rational, the intellectual, is bounded on both sides by the illimitable, the unknowable, the ever unknown. Herein is the search, herein are the inquiries, here are the facts; from this comes the light which is known to the world as religion. Essentially, however, religion belongs to the supersensuous and not to the sense plane. It is beyond all reasoning and is not on the plane of intellect. It is a vision, an inspiration, a plunge into the unknown and unknowable, making the unknowable more than known for it can never be "known". This search has been in the human mind, as I believe, from the very beginning of humanity. There cannot have been human reasoning and intellect in any period of the world's history without this struggle, this search beyond. In our little universe, this human mind, we see a thought arise. Whence it arises we do not know; and when it disappears, where it goes, we know not either. The macrocosm and the microcosm are, as it were, in the same groove, passing through the same stages, vibrating in the same key.

I shall try to bring before you the Hindu theory that religions do not come from without, but from within. It is my belief that religious thought is in man's very constitution, so much so that it is impossible for him to give up religion until he can give up his mind and body, until he can give up thought and life. As long as a man thinks, this struggle must go on, and so long man must have some form of religion. Thus we see various forms of religion in the world. It is a bewildering study; but it is not, as many of us think, a vain speculation. Amidst this chaos there is harmony, throughout these discordant sounds there is a note of concord; and he who is prepared to listen to it will catch the tone.

The great question of all questions at the present time is this: Taking for granted that the known and the knowable are bounded on both sides by the unknowable and the infinitely unknown, why struggle for that infinite unknown? Why shall we not be content with the known? Why shall we not rest satisfied with eating, drinking, and doing a little good to society? This idea is in the air. From the most learned professor to the prattling baby, we are told that to do good to the world is all of religion, and that it is useless to trouble ourselves about questions of the beyond. So much is this the case that it has become a truism.

But fortunately we must inquire into the beyond. This present, this expressed, is only one part of that unexpressed. The sense universe is, as it were, only one portion, one bit of that infinite spiritual universe projected into the plane of sense consciousness. How can this little bit of projection be explained, be understood, without. Knowing that which is beyond? It is said of Socrates that one day while lecturing at Athens, he met a Brahmin who had travelled into Greece, and Socrates told the Brahmin that the greatest study for mankind is man. The Brahmin sharply retorted: "How can you know man until you know Gods" This God, this eternally Unknowable, or Absolute, or Infinite, or without name – you may call Him by what name you like – is the rationale, the only explanation, the raison d'être of that which is known and knowable, this present life. Take anything before you, the most material thing – take one of the most material sciences, as chemistry or physics, astronomy or biology – study it, push the study forward and forward, and the gross forms will begin to melt and become finer and finer, until they come to a point where you are bound to make a tremendous leap from these material things into the immaterial. The gross melts into the fine, physics into metaphysics, in every department of knowledge.

Thus man finds himself driven to a study of the beyond. Life will be a desert, human life will be vain, if we cannot know the beyond. It is very well to say: Be contented with the things of the present. The cows and the dogs are, and so are all animals; and that is what makes them animals. So if man rests content with the present and gives up all search into the beyond, mankind will have to go back to the animal plane again. It is religion, the inquiry into the beyond, that makes the difference between man and an animal. Well has it been said that man is the only animal that naturally looks upwards; every other animal naturally looks down. That looking upward and going upward and seeking perfection are what is called salvation; and the sooner a man begins to go higher, the sooner he raises himself towards this idea of truth as salvation. It does not consist in the amount of money in your pocket, or the dress you wear, or the house you live in, but in the wealth of spiritual thought in your brain. That is what makes for human progress, that is the source of all material and intellectual progress, the motive power behind, the enthusiasm that pushes mankind forward.

Religion does not live on bread, does not dwell in a house. Again and again you hear this objection advanced: "What good can religion do? Can it take away the poverty of the poor?" Supposing it cannot, would that prove the untruth of religion? Suppose a baby stands up among you when you are trying to demonstrate an astronomical theorem, and says, "Does it bring gingerbread?" "No, it does not", you answer. "Then," says the baby, "it is useless." Babies judge the whole universe from their own standpoint, that of producing gingerbread, and so do the babies of the world. We must not judge of higher things from a low standpoint. Everything must be judged by its own standard and the infinite must be judged by the standard of infinity. Religion permeates the whole of man's life, not only the present, but the past, present, and future. It is, therefore, the eternal relation between the eternal soul and the eternal God. Is it logical to measure its value by its action upon five minutes of human life? Certainly not. These are all negative arguments.

Now comes the question: Can religion really accomplish anything? It can. It brings to man eternal life. It has made man what he is, and will make of this human animal a god. That is what religion can do. Take religion from human society and what will remain? Nothing but a forest of brutes. Sense-happiness is not the goal of humanity. Wisdom (Jnâna) is the goal of all life. We find that man enjoys his intellect more than an animal enjoys its senses; and we see that man enjoys his spiritual nature even more than his rational nature. So the highest wisdom must be this spiritual knowledge. With this knowledge will come bliss. All these things of this world are but the shadows, the manifestations in the third or fourth degree of the real Knowledge and Bliss.

One question more: What is the goal? Nowadays it is asserted that man is infinitely progressing, forward and forward, and there is no goal of perfection to attain to. Ever approaching, never attaining, whatever that may mean and however wonderful it may be, it is absurd on the face of it. Is there any motion in a straight line? A straight line infinitely projected becomes a circle, it returns to the starting point. You must end where you begin; and as you began in God, you must go back to God. What remains? Detail work. Through eternity you have to do the detail work.

Yet another question: Are we to discover new truths of religion as we go on? Yea and nay. In the first place, we cannot know anything more of religion, it has all been known. In all religions of the world you will find it claimed that there is a unity within us.

Being one with divinity, there cannot be any further progress in that sense. Knowledge means finding this unity. I see you as men and women, and this is variety. It becomes scientific knowledge when I group you together and call you human beings. Take the science of chemistry, for instance. Chemists are seeking to resolve all known substances into their original elements, and if possible, to find the one element from which all these are derived. The time may come when they will find one element that is the source of all other elements. Reaching that, they can go no further; the science of chemistry will have become perfect. So it is with the science of religion. If we can discover this perfect unity, there cannot be any further progress.

The next question is: Can such a unity be found? In India the attempt has been made from the earliest times to reach a science of religion and philosophy, for the Hindus do not separate these as is customary in Western countries. We regard religion and philosophy as but two aspects of one thing which must equally be grounded in reason and scientific truth.

The system of the Sânkhya philosophy is one of the most ancient in India, or in fact in the world. Its great exponent Kapila is the father of all Hindu psychology; and the ancient system that he taught is still the foundation of all accepted systems of philosophy in India today which are known as the Darshanas. They all adopt his psychology, however widely they differ in other respects.

The Vedanta, as the logical outcome of the Sankhya, pushes its conclusions yet further. While its cosmology agrees with that taught by Kapila, the Vedanta is not satisfied to end in dualism, but continues its search for the final unity which is alike the goal of science and religion.

❑

Bhakti

(Delivered at Sialkote, Punjab)

In response to invitations from the Punjab and Kashmir, the Swami Vivekananda travelled through those parts. He stayed in Kashmir for over a month and his work there was very much appreciated by the Maharaja and his brothers. He then spent a few days in visiting Murree, Rawalpindi, and Jammu, and at each of these places he delivered lectures. Subsequently he visited Sialkote and lectured twice, once in English and once in Hindi. The subject of the Swamiji's Hindi lecture was Bhakti, a summary of which, translated into English, is given below:

The various religions that exist in the world, although they differ in the form of worship they take, are really one. In some places the people build temples and worship in them, in some they worship fire, in others they prostrate themselves before idols, while there are many who do not believe at all in God. All are true, for, if you look to the real spirit, the real religion, and the truths in each of them, they are all alike. In some religions God is not worshipped, nay, His existence is not believed in, but good and worthy men are worshipped as if they were Gods. The example worthy of citation in this case is Buddhism. Bhakti is everywhere, whether directed to God or to noble persons. Upâsâna in the form of Bhakti is everywhere supreme, and Bhakti is more easily attained than Jnâna. The latter requires favourable circumstances and strenuous practice. Yoga cannot be properly practiced unless a man is physically very healthy and free from all worldly attachments. But Bhakti can be more easily practiced by persons in every condition of life. Shândilya Rishi, who wrote about Bhakti, says that extreme love for God is Bhakti. Prahlâda speaks to the same effect. If a man does not get food one day, he is troubled; if his son dies, how agonising it is to him! The true Bhakta feels the same pangs in his heart when he yearns after God. The great quality of Bhakti is that it cleanses the mind, and the firmly established Bhakti for the Supreme Lord is alone sufficient to purify the mind. "O God, Thy names are innumerable, but in every name Thy power is manifest, and every name is pregnant with deep and mighty significance." We should think of God always and not consider time and place for doing so.

The different names under which God is worshipped are apparently different. One thinks that his method of worshipping God is the most efficacious, and another thinks that his is the more potent process of attaining salvation. But look at the true basis of all, and it is one. The Shaivas call Shiva the most powerful; the Vaishnavas hold to their all-powerful Vishnu; the worshippers of Devi will not yield to any in their idea that their Devi is the most omnipotent power in the universe. Leave inimical thoughts aside if you want to have permanent Bhakti. Hatred is a thing which greatly impedes the course of Bhakti, and the man who hates none reaches God. Even then the devotion for one's own ideal is necessary. Hanumân says, "Vishnu and Râma, I know, are one and the same, but after all, the lotus-cyed Rama is my best treasure." The peculiar tendencies with which a person is born must remain with him. That is the chief reason why the world cannot be of one religion – and God forbid that there should be one religion only – for the world would then be a chaos and not a cosmos. A man must follow the tendencies peculiar to himself; and if he gets a teacher to help him to advance along his own lines, he will progress.

We should let a person go the way he intends to go, but if we try to force him into another path, he will lose what he has already attained and will become worthless. As the face of one person does not resemble that of another, so the nature of one differs from that of another, and why should he not be allowed to act accordingly? A river flows in a certain direction; and if you direct the course into a regular channel, the current becomes more rapid and the force is increased, but try to divert it from its proper course, and you will see the result; the volume as well as the force will be lessened. This life is very important, and it, therefore, ought to be guided in the way one's tendency prompts him. In India there was no enmity, and every religion was left unmolested; so religion has lived. It ought to be remembered that quarrels about religion arise from thinking that one alone has the truth and whoever does not believe as one does is a fool; while another thinks that the other is a hypocrite, for if he were not one, he would follow him.

If God wished that people should follow one religion, why have so many religions sprung up? Methods have been vainly tried to force one religion upon everyone. Even when the sword was lifted to make all people follow one religion, history tells us that ten religions sprang up in its place. One religion cannot suit all. Man is the product of two forces, action and reaction, which make him think. If such forces did not exercise a man's mind, he would be incapable of thinking. Man is a creature who thinks; Manushya (man) is a being with Manas (mind); and as soon as his thinking power goes, he becomes no better than an animal. Who would like such a man? God forbid that any such state should come upon the people of India. Variety in unity is necessary to keep man as man. Variety ought to be preserved in everything; for as long as there is variety the world will exist. Of course variety does not merely mean that one is small and the other is great; but if all play their parts equally well in their respective position in life, the variety is still preserved. In every religion there have been men good and able, thus making the religion to which they belonged worthy of respect; and as there are such people in every religion, there ought to be no hatred for any sect whatsoever.

Then the question may be asked, should we respect that religion which advocates vice? The answer will be certainly in the negative, and such a religion ought to be expelled at once, because it is productive of harm. All religion is to be based upon morality, and personal purity is to be counted superior to Dharma. In this connection it ought to be known that Âchâra means purity inside and outside. External purity can be attained by cleansing the body with water and other things which are recommended in the Shâstras. The internal man is to be purified by not speaking falsehood, by not drinking, by not doing immoral acts, and by doing good to others. If you do not commit any sin, if you do not tell lies, if you do not drink, gamble, or commit theft, it is good. But that is only your duty and you cannot be applauded for it. Some service to others is also to be done. As you do good to yourself, so you must do good to others.

Here I shall say something about food regulations. All the old customs have faded away, and nothing but a vague notion of not eating with this man and not eating; with that man has been left among our countrymen. Purity by touch is the only relic left of the good rules laid down hundreds of years ago. Three kinds of food are forbidden in the Shastras. First, the food that is by its very nature defective, as garlic or onions. If a man eats too much of them it creates passion, and he may be led to commit immoralities, hateful both to God and man. Secondly, food contaminated by external impurities. We ought to select some place quite neat and clean in which to keep our food. Thirdly, we should avoid eating food touched by a wicked man, because contact with such produces bad ideas in us. Even if one be a son of a Brahmin, but is profligate and immoral in his habits, we should not eat food from his hands.

But the spirit of these observances is gone. What is left is this, that we cannot eat from the hands of any man who is not of the highest caste, even though he be the most wise and holy person. The disregard of those old rules is ever to be found in the confectioner's shop. If you look there, you will find flies hovering all over the confectionery, and the dust from the road blowing upon the sweet¬meats, and the confectioner himself in a dress that is not very clean and neat. Purchasers should declare with one voice that they will not buy sweets unless they are kept in glass-cases in the Halwai's shop. That would have the salutary effect of preventing flies from conveying cholera and other plague germs to the sweets. We ought to improve, but instead of improving we have gone back. Manu says that we should not spit in water, but we throw all sorts of filth into the rivers. Considering all these things we find that the purification of one's outer self is very necessary. The Shâstrakâras knew that very well. But now the real spirit of this observance of purity about food is lost and the letter only remains. Thieves, drunkards, and criminals can be our caste-fellows, but if a good and noble man eats food with a person of a lower caste, who is quite as respectable as himself, he will be outcasted and lost for ever. This custom has been the bane of our country. It ought, therefore, to be distinctly understood that sin is incurred by coming in contact with sinners, and nobility in the company of good persons; and keeping aloof from the wicked is the external purification.

The internal purification is a task much more severe. It consists in speaking the truth, sensing the poor, helping the needy, etc. Do we always speak the truth? What happens is often this. People go to the house of a rich person for some business of their own and flatter him by calling him benefactor of the poor and so forth, even though that man may cut the throat of a poor man coming to his house. What is this? Nothing but falsehood. And it is this that pollutes the mind. It is therefore, truly said that whatever a man says who has purified his inner self for twelve years without entertaining a single vicious idea during that period is sure to come true. This is the power of truth, and one who has cleansed both the inner and the outer self is alone capable of Bhakti. But the beauty is that Bhakti itself cleanses the mind to a great extent. Although the Jews, Mohammedans, and Christians do not set so much importance upon the excessive external purification of the body as the Hindus do, still they have it in some form or other; they find that to a certain extent it is always required. Among the Jews, idol-worship is condemned, but they had a temple in which was kept a chest which they called an ark, in which the Tables of the Law were preserved, and above the chest were two figures of angels with wings outstretched, between which the Divine Presence was supposed to manifest itself as a cloud. That temple has long since been destroyed, but the new temples are made exactly after the old fashion, and in the chest religious books are kept. The Roman Catholics and the Greek Christians have idol-worship in certain forms. The image of Jesus and that of his mother are worshipped. Among Protestants there is no idol-worship, yet they worship God in a personal form, which may be called idol-worship in another form. Among Parsees and Iranians fire-worship is carried on to a great extent. Among Mohammedans the prophets and great and noble persons are worshipped, and they turn their faces towards the Caaba when they pray. These things show that men at the first stage of religious development have to make use of something external, and when the inner self becomes purified they turn to more abstract conceptions. "When the Jiva is sought to be united with Brahman it is best, when meditation is practiced it is mediocre, repetition of names is the lowest form, and external worship is the lowest of the low." But it should be distinctly understood that even in practicing the last there is no sin. Everybody ought to do what he is able to do; and if he be dissuaded from that, he will do it in some other way in order to attain his end. So we should not speak ill of a man who worships idols. He is in that stage of growth, and, therefore, must have them; wise men should try to help forward such men and get them to do better. But there is no use in quarrelling about these various sorts of worship.

Some persons worship God for the sake of obtaining wealth, others because they want to have a son, and they think themselves Bhâgavatas (devotees). This is no Bhakti, and they are not true Bhagavatas. When a Sâdhu comes who professes that he can make gold, they run to him, and they still consider themselves Bhagavatas. It is not Bhakti if we worship God with the desire for a son; it is not Bhakti if we worship with the desire to be rich; it is not Bhakti even if we have a desire for heaven; it is not Bhakti if a man worships with the desire of being saved from the tortures of hell. Bhakti is not the outcome of fear or greediness. He is the true Bhagavata who says, "O God, I do not want a beautiful wife, I do not want knowledge or salvation. Let me be born and die hundreds of times. What I want is that I should be ever engaged in Thy service." It is at this stage – and when a man sees God in everything, and everything in God – that he attains perfect Bhakti. It is then that he sees Vishnu incarnated in everything from the microbe to Brahmâ, and it is then that he sees God manifesting Himself in everything, it is then that he feels that there is nothing without God, and it is then and then alone that thinking himself to be the most insignificant of all beings he worships God with the true spirit of a Bhakta. He then leaves Tirthas and external forms of worship far behind him, he sees every man to be the most perfect temple.

Bhakti is described in several ways in the Shastras. We say that God is our Father. In the same way we call Him Mother, and so on. These relationships are conceived in order to strengthen Bhakti in us, and they make us feel nearer and dearer to God. Hence these names are justifiable in one way, and that is that the words are simply words of endearment, the outcome of the fond love which a true Bhagavata feels for God. Take the story of Râdhâ and Krishna in Râsalilâ. The story simply exemplifies the true spirit of a Bhakta, because no love in the world exceeds that existing between a man and a woman. When there is such intense love, there is no fear, no other attachment save that one which binds that pair in an inseparable and all-absorbing bond. But with regard to parents, love is accompanied with fear due to the reverence we have for them. Why should we care whether God created anything or not, what have we to do with the fact that He is our preserver? He is only our Beloved, and we should adore Him devoid all thoughts of fear. A man loves God only when he has no other desire, when he thinks of nothing else and when he is mad after Him. That love which a man has for his beloved can illustrate the love we ought to have for God. Krishna is the God and Radha loves Him; read those books which describe that story, and then you can imagine the way you should love God. But how many understand this? How can people who are vicious to their very core and have no idea of what morality is understand all this? When people drive all sorts of worldly thoughts from their minds and live in a clear moral and spiritual atmosphere, it is then that they understand the abstrusest of thoughts even if they be uneducated. But how few are there of that nature! There is not a single religion which cannot be perverted by man. For example, he may think that the Âtman is quite separate from the body, and so, when committing sins with the body his Atman is unaffected. If religions were truly followed, there would not have been a single man, whether Hindu, Mohammedan, or Christian, who would not have been all purity. But men are guided by their own nature, whether good or bad; there is no gainsaying that. But in the world, there are always some who get intoxicated when they hear of God, and shed tears of joy when they read of God. Such men are true Bhaktas.

At the initial stage of religious development a man thinks of God as his Master and himself as His servant. He feels indebted to Him for providing for his daily wants, and so forth. Put such thoughts aside. There is but one attractive power, and that is God; and it is in obedience to that attractive power that the sun and the moon and everything else move. Everything in this world, whether good or bad, belongs to God. Whatever occurs in our life, whether good or bad, is bringing us to Him. One man kills another because of some selfish purpose. But the motive behind is love, whether for himself or for any one else. Whether we do good or evil, the propeller is love. When a tiger kills a buffalo, it is because he or his cubs are hungry.

God is love personified. He is apparent in everything. Everybody is being drawn to Him whether he knows it or not. When a woman loves her husband, she does not understand that it is the divine in her husband that is the great attractive power. The God of Love is the one thing to be worshipped. So long as we think of Him only as the Creator and Preserver, we can offer Him external worship, but when we get beyond all that and think Him to be Love Incarnate, seeing Him in all things and all things in Him, it is then that supreme Bhakti is attained.

❑

On Lord Buddha

(Delivered in Detroit)

In every religion we find one type of self-devotion particularly developed. The type of working without a motive is most highly developed in Buddhism. Do not mistake Buddhism and Brâhminism. In this country you are very apt to do so. Buddhism is one of our sects. It was founded by a great man called Gautama, who became disgusted at the eternal metaphysical discussions of his day, and the cumbrous rituals, and more especially with the caste system. Some people say that we are born to a certain state, and therefore we are superior to others who are not thus born. He was also against the tremendous priestcraft. He preached a religion in which there was no motive power, and was perfectly agnostic about metaphysics or theories about God. He was often asked if there was a God, and he answered, he did not know. When asked about right conduct, he would reply, "Do good and be good." There came five Brâhmins, who asked him to settle their discussion. One said, "Sir, my book says that God is such and such, and that this is the way to come to God." Another said, "That is wrong, for my book says such and such, and this is the way to come to God"; and so the others. He listened calmly to all of them, and then asked them one by one, "Does any one of your books say that God becomes angry, that He ever injures anyone, that He is impure?" "No, Sir, they all teach that God is pure and good." "Then, my friends, why do you not become pure and good first, that you may know what God is?"

Of course I do not endorse all his philosophy. I want a good deal of metaphysics, for myself. I entirely differ in many respects, but, because I differ, is that any reason why I should not see the beauty of the man? He was the only man who was bereft of all motive power. There were other great men who all said they were the Incarnations of God Himself, and that those who would believe in them would go to heaven. But what did Buddha say with his dying breath? "None can help you; help yourself; work out your own salvation." He said about himself, "Buddha is the name of infinite knowledge, infinite as the sky; I, Gautama, have reached that state; you will all reach that too if you struggle for it." Bereft of all motive power, he did not want to go to heaven, did not want money; he gave up his throne and everything else and went about begging his bread through the streets of India, preaching for the good of men and animals with a heart as wide as the ocean.

He was the only man who was ever ready to give up his life for animals to stop a sacrifice. He once said to a king, "If the sacrifice of a lamb helps you to go to heaven, sacrificing a man will help you better; so sacrifice me." The king was astonished. And yet this man was without any motive power. He stands as the perfection of the active type, and the very height to which he attained shows that through the power of work we can also attain to the highest spirituality.

To many the path becomes easier if they believe in God. But the life of Buddha shows that even a man who does not believe in God, has no metaphysics, belongs to no sect, and does not go to any church, or temple, and is a confessed materialist, even he can attain to the highest. We have no right to judge him. I wish I had one infinitesimal part of Buddha's heart. Buddha may or may not have believed in God; that does not matter to me. He reached the same state of perfection to which others come by Bhakti – love of God – Yoga, or Jnâna. Perfection does not come from belief or faith. Talk does not count for anything. Parrots can do that. Perfection comes through the disinterested performance of action.

❑

The Ramayana

(Delivered at the Shakespeare Club, Pasadena, California, on January 31, 1900)

There are two great epics in the Sanskrit language, which are very ancient. Of course, there are hundreds of other epic poems. The Sanskrit language and literature have been continued down to the present day, although, for more than two thousand years, it has ceased to be a spoken language. I am now going to speak to you of the two most ancient epics, called the Râmâyana and the Mahâbhârata.

They embody the manners and customs, the state of society, civilisation, etc., of the ancient Indians. The oldest of these epics is called Ramayana, "The Life of Râma". There was some poetical literature before this – most of the Vedas, the sacred books of the Hindus, are written in a sort of metre – but this book is held by common consent in India as the very beginning of poetry.

The name of the poet or sage was Vâlmiki. Later on, a great many poetical stories were fastened upon that ancient poet; and subsequently, it became a very general practice to attribute to his authorship very many verses that were not his. Notwithstanding all these interpolations, it comes down to us as a very beautiful arrangement, without equal in the literatures of the world.

There was a young man that could not in any way support his family. He was strong and vigorous and, finally, became a highway robber; he attacked persons in the street and robbed them, and with that money he supported his father, mother, wife, and children. This went on continually, until one day a great saint called Nârada was passing by, and the robber attacked him. The sage asked the robber, "Why are you going to rob me? It is a great sin to rob human beings and kill them. What do you incur all this sin for?" The robber said, "Why, I want to support my family with this money." "Now", said the sage, "do you think that they take a share of your sin also?" "Certainly they do," replied the robber. "Very good," said the sage, "make me safe by tying me up here, while you go home and ask your people whether they will share your sin in the same way as they share the money you make." The man accordingly went to his father, and asked, "Father, do you know how I support you?" He answered, "No, I do not." "I am a robber, and I kill persons and rob them." "What! you do that, my son? Get away! You outcast! "He then went to his mother and asked her, "Mother, do you know how I support you?" "No," she replied. "Through robbery and murder." "How horrible it is!"

cried the mother. "But, do you partake in my sin?" said the son. "Why should I? I never committed a robbery," answered the mother. Then, he went to his wife and questioned her, "Do you know how I maintain you all?" "No," she responded. "Why, I am a highwayman," he rejoined, "and for years have been robbing people; that is how I support and maintain you all. And what I now want to know is, whether you are ready to share in my sin." "By no means. You are my husband, and it is your duty to support me."

The eyes of the robber were opened. "That is the way of the world – even my nearest relatives, for whom I have been robbing, will not share in my destiny." He came back to the place where he had bound the sage, unfastened his bonds, fell at his feet, recounted everything and said, "Save me! What can I do?" The sage said, "Give up your present course of life. You see that none of your family really loves you, so give up all these delusions. They will share your prosperity; but the moment you have nothing, they will desert you. There is none who will share in your evil, but they will all share in your good. Therefore worship Him who alone stands by us whether we are doing good or evil. He never leaves us, for love never drags down, knows no barter, no selfishness."

Then the sage taught him how to worship. And this man left everything and went into a forest. There he went on praying and meditating until he forgot himself so entirely that the ants came and built ant-hills around him and he was quite unconscious of it. After many years had passed, a voice came saying, "Arise, O sage!" Thus aroused he exclaimed, "Sage? I am a robber!"

"No more 'robber'," answered the voice, "a purified sage art thou. Thine old name is gone. But now, since thy meditation was so deep and great that thou didst not remark even the ant-hills which surrounded thee, henceforth, thy name shall be Valmiki – 'he that was born in the ant-hill'." So, he became a sage.

And this is how he became a poet. One day as this sage, Valmiki, was going to bathe in the holy river Ganga, he saw a pair of doves wheeling round and round, and kissing each other. The sage looked up and was pleased at the sight, but in a second an arrow whisked past him and killed the male dove. As the dove fell down on the ground, the female dove went on whirling round and round the dead body of its companion in grief. In a moment the poet became miserable, and looking round, he saw the hunter. "Thou art a wretch," he cried, "without the smallest mercy! Thy slaying hand would not even stop for love!"

"What is this? What am I saying?" the poet thought to himself, "I have never spoken in this sort of way before." And then a voice came: "Be not afraid. This is poetry that is coming out of your mouth. Write the life of Rama in poetic language for the benefit of the world." And that is how the poem first began. The first verse sprang out of pits from the mouth of Valmiki, the first poet. And it was after that, that he wrote the beautiful Ramayana, "The Life of Rama".

There was an ancient Indian town called Ayodhyâ – and it exists even in modern times. The province in which it is still located is called Oudh, and most of you may have noticed it in the map of India. That was the ancient Ayodhya. There, in ancient times, reigned a king called Dasharatha. He had three queens, but the king had not any children by them. And like good Hindus, the king and the queens, all went on pilgrimages fasting and praying, that they might have children and, in good time, four sons were born. The eldest of them was Rama.

Now, as it should be, these four brothers were thoroughly educated in all branches of learning. To avoid future quarrels there was in ancient India a custom for the king in his own lifetime to nominate his eldest son as his successor, the Yuvarâja, young king, as he is called.

Now, there was another king, called Janaka, and this king had a beautiful daughter named Sitâ. Sita was found in a field; she was a daughter of the Earth, and was born without parents. The word "Sita" in ancient Sanskrit means the furrow made by a plough. In the ancient mythology of India you will find persons born of one parent only, or persons born without parents, born of sacrificial fire, born in the field, and so on – dropped from the clouds as it were. All those sorts of miraculous birth were common in the mythological lore of India.

Sita, being the daughter of the Earth, was pure and immaculate. She was brought up by King Janaka. When she was of a marriageable age, the king wanted to find a suitable husband for her.

There was an ancient Indian custom called Svayamvara, by which the princesses used to choose husbands. A number of princes from different parts of the country were invited, and the princess in splendid array, with a garland in her hand, and accompanied by a crier who enumerated the distinctive claims of each of the royal suitors, would pass in the midst of those assembled before her, and select the prince she liked for her husband by throwing the garland of flowers round his neck. They would then be married with much pomp and grandeur.

There were numbers of princes who aspired for the hand of Sita; the test demanded on this occasion was the breaking of a huge bow, called Haradhanu. All the princes put forth all their strength to accomplish this feat, but failed. Finally, Rama took the mighty bow in his hands and with easy grace broke it in twain. Thus Sita selected Rama, the son of King Dasharatha for her husband, and they were wedded with great rejoicings. Then, Rama took his bride to his home, and his old father thought that the time was now come for him to retire and appoint Rama as Yuvaraja. Everything was accordingly made ready for the ceremony, and the whole country was jubilant over the affair, when the younger queen Kaikeyi was reminded by one of her maidservants of two promises made to her by the king long ago. At one time she had pleased the king very much, and he offered to grant her two boons: "Ask any two things in my power and I will grant them to you," said he, but she made no request then. She had forgotten all about it; but the evil-minded maidservant in her employ began to work upon her jealousy with regard to Rama being installed on the throne, and insinuated to her how nice it would be for her if her own son had succeeded the king, until the queen was almost mad with jealousy. Then the servant suggested to her to ask from the king the two promised boons: one would be that her own son Bharata should be placed on the throne, and the other, that Rama should be sent to the forest and be exiled for fourteen years.

Now, Rama was the life and soul of the old king and when this wicked request was made to him, he as a king felt he could not go back on his word. So he did not know what to do. But Rama came to the rescue and willingly offered to give up the throne and go into exile, so that his father might not be guilty of falsehood. So Rama went into exile for fourteen years, accompanied by his loving wife Sita and his devoted brother Lakshmana, who would on no account be parted from him.

The Aryans did not know who were the inhabitants of these wild forests. In those days the forest tribes they called "monkeys", and some of the so-called "monkeys", if unusually strong and powerful, were called "demons".

So, into the forest, inhabited by demons and monkeys, Rama, Lakshmana, and Sita went. When Sita had offered to accompany Rama, he exclaimed, "How can you, a princess, face hardships and accompany me into a forest full of unknown dangers!"

But Sita replied, "Wherever Rama goes, there goes Sita. How can you talk of 'princess' and 'royal birth' to me? I go before you!"

So, Sita went. And the younger brother, he also went with them. They penetrated far into the forest, until they reached the river Godâvari. On the banks of the river they built little cottages, and Rama and Lakshmana used to hunt deer and collect fruits. After they had lived thus for some time, one day there came a demon giantess. She was the sister of the giant king of Lanka (Ceylon). Roaming through the forest at will, she came across Rama, and seeing that he was a very handsome man, she fell in love with him at once. But Rama was the purest of men, and also he was a married man; so of course he could not return her love. In revenge, she went to her brother, the giant king, and told him all about the beautiful Sita, the wife of Rama.

Rama was the most powerful of mortals; there were no giants or demons or anybody else strong enough to conquer him. So, the giant king had to resort to subterfuge. He got hold of another giant who was a magician and changed him into a beautiful golden deer; and the deer went prancing round about the place where Rama lived, until Sita was fascinated by its beauty and asked Rama to go and capture the deer for her. Rama went into the forest to catch the deer, leaving his brother in charge of Sita. Then Lakshmana laid a circle of fire round the cottage, and he said to Sita, "Today I see something may befall you; and, therefore, I tell you not to go outside of this magic circle. Some danger may befall you if you do."

In the meanwhile, Rama had pierced the magic deer with his arrow, and immediately the deer, changed into the form of a man, died.

Immediately, at the cottage was heard the voice of Rama, crying, "Oh, Lakshmana, come to my help!"

and Sita said, "Lakshmana, go at once into the forest to help Rama! "That is not Rama's voice," protested Lakshmana. But at the entreaties of Sita, Lakshmana had to go in search of Rama. As soon as he went away, the giant king, who had taken the form of a mendicant monk, stood at the gate and asked for alms. "Wait awhile," said Sita, "until my husband comes back and I will give you plentiful alms." "I cannot wait, good lady," said he, "I am very hungry, give me anything you have." At this, Sita, who had a few fruits in the cottage, brought them out. But the mendicant monk after many persuasions prevailed upon her to bring the alms to him, assuring her that she need have no fear as he was a holy person. So Sita came out of the magic circle, and immediately the seeming monk assumed his giant body, and grasping Sita in his arms he called his magic chariot, and putting her therein, he fled with the weeping Sita. Poor Sita! She was utterly helpless, nobody, was there to come to her aid. As the giant was carrying her away, she took off a few of the ornaments from her arms and at intervals dropped them to the grounds

She was taken by Râvana to his kingdom, Lanka, the island of Ceylon. He made peals to her to become his queen, and tempted her in many ways to accede to his request. But Sita who was chastity itself, would not even speak to the giant; and he to punish her, made her live under a tree, day and night, until she should consent to be his wife.

When Rama and Lakshmana returned to the cottage and found that Sita was not there, their grief knew no bounds. They could not imagine what had become of her. The two brothers went on, seeking, seeking everywhere for Sita, but could find no trace of her. After long searching, they came across a group of "monkeys", and in the midst of them was Hanumân, the "divine monkey". Hanuman, the best of the monkeys, became the most faithful servant of Rama and helped him in rescuing Sita, as we shall see later on. His devotion to Rama was so great that he is still worshipped by the Hindus as the ideal of a true servant of the Lord. You see, by the "monkeys" and "demons" are meant the aborigines of South India.

So, Rama, at last, fell in with these monkeys. They told him that they had seen flying through the sky a chariot, in which was seated a demon who was carrying away a most beautiful lady, and that she was weeping bitterly, and as the chariot passed over their heads she dropped one of her ornaments to attract their attention. Then they showed Rama the ornament. Lakshmana took up the ornament, and said, “I do not know whose ornament this is.” Rama took it from him and recognised it at once, saying, “Yes, it is Sita’s.” Lakshmana could not recognise the ornament, because in India the wife of the elder brother was held in so much reverence that he had never looked upon the arms and the neck of Sita. So you see, as it was a necklace, he did not know whose it was. There is in this episode a touch of the old Indian custom. Then, the monkeys told Rama who this demon king was and where he lived, and then they all went to seek for him.

Now, the monkey-king Vâli and his younger brother Sugriva were then fighting amongst themselves for the kingdom. The younger brother was helped by Rama, and he regained the kingdom from Vali, who had driven him away; and he, in return, promised to help Rama. They searched the country all round, but could not find Sita. At last Hanuman leaped by one bound from the coast of India to the island of Ceylon, and there went looking all over Lanka for Sita, but nowhere could he find her.

You see, this giant king had conquered the gods, the men, in fact the whole world; and he had collected all the beautiful women and made them his concubines. So, Hanuman thought to himself, “Sita cannot be with them in the palace. She would rather die than be in such a place." So Hanuman went to seek for her elsewhere. At last, he found Sita under a tree, pale and thin, like the new moon that lies low in the horizon. Now Hanuman took the form of a little monkey and settled on the tree, and there he witnessed how giantesses sent by Ravana came and tried to frighten Sita into submission, but she would not even listen to the name of the giant king.

Then, Hanuman came nearer to Sita and told her how he became the messenger of Rama, who had sent him to find out where Sita was; and Hanuman showed to Sita the signet ring which Rama had given as a token for establishing his identity. He also informed her that as soon as Rama would know her whereabouts, he would come with an army and conquer the giant and recover her. However, he suggested to Sita that if she wished it, he would take her on his shoulders and could with one leap clear the ocean and get back to Rama. But Sita could not bear the idea, as she was chastity itself, and could not touch the body of any man except her husband. So, Sita remained where she was. But she gave him a jewel from her hair to carry to Rama; and with that Hanuman returned.

Learning everything about Sita from Hanuman, Rama collected an army, and with it marched towards the southernmost point of India. There Rama's monkeys built a huge bridge, called Setu-

Bandha, connecting India with Ceylon. In very low water even now it is possible to cross from India to Ceylon over the sand-banks there.

Now Rama was God incarnate, otherwise, how could he have done all these things? He was an Incarnation of God, according to the Hindus. They in India believe him to be the seventh Incarnation of God.

The monkeys removed whole hills, placed them in the sea and covered them with stones and trees, thus making a huge embankment. A little squirrel, so it is said, was there rolling himself in the sand and running backwards and forwards on to the bridge and shaking himself. Thus in his small way he was working for the bridge of Rama by putting in sand. The monkeys laughed, for they were bringing whole mountains, whole forests, huge loads of sand for the bridge – so they laughed at the little squirrel rolling in the sand and then shaking himself. But Rama saw it and remarked: "Blessed be the little squirrel; he is doing his work to the best of his ability, and he is therefore quite as great as the greatest of you." Then he gently stroked the squirrel on the back, and the marks of Rama's fingers, running lengthways, are seen on the squirrel's back to this day.

Now, when the bridge was finished, the whole army of monkeys, led by Rama and his brother entered

Ceylon. For several months afterwards tremendous war and bloodshed followed. At last, this demon king, Ravana, was conquered and killed; and his capital, with all the palaces and everything, which were entirely of solid gold, was taken. In far-away villages in the interior of India, when I tell them that I have been in Ceylon, the simple folk say, "There, as our books tell, the houses are built of gold." So, all these golden cities fell into the hands of Rama, who gave them over to Vibhishana, the younger brother of Ravana, and seated him on the throne in the place of his brother, as a return for the valuable services rendered by him to Rama during the war.

Then Rama with Sita and his followers left Lanka. But there ran a murmur among the followers. "The test! The test!"

They cried, "Sita has not given the test that she was perfectly pure in Ravana's household." "Pure! she is chastity itself" exclaimed Rama. "Never mind! We want the test," persisted the people. Subsequently, a huge sacrificial fire was made ready, into which Sita had to plunge herself. Rama was in agony, thinking that Sita was lost; but in a moment, the God of fire himself appeared with a throne upon his head, and upon the throne was Sita. Then, there was universal rejoicing, and everybody was satisfied.

Early during the period of exile, Bharata, the younger brother had come and informed Rama, of the death of the old king and vehemently insisted on his occupying the throne. During Rama's exile Bharata would on no account ascend the throne and out of respect placed a pair of Rama's wooden shoes on it as a substitute for his brother. Then Rama returned to his capital, and by the common consent of his people he became the king of Ayodhya.

After Rama regained his kingdom, he took the necessary vows which in olden times the king had to take for the benefit of his people. The king was the slave of his people, and had to bow to public opinion, as we shall see later on. Rama passed a few years in happiness with Sita, when the people again began to murmur that Sita had been stolen by a demon and carried across the ocean. They were not satisfied with the former test and clamoured for another test, otherwise she must be banished.

In order to satisfy the demands of the people, Sita was banished, and left to live in the forest, where was the hermitage of the sage and poet Valmiki. The sage found poor Sita weeping and forlorn, and hearing her sad story, sheltered her in his Âshrama. Sita was expecting soon to become a mother, and she gave birth to twin boys. The poet never told the children who they were. He brought them up together in the Brahmachârin life. He then composed the poem known as Ramayana, set it to music, and dramatized it.

The drama, in India, was a very holy thing. Drama and music are themselves held to be religion. Any song – whether it be a love-song or otherwise – if one's whole soul is in that song, one attains salvation, one has nothing else to do. They say it leads to the same goal as meditation.

So, Valmiki dramatised "The Life of Rama", and taught Rama's two children how to recite and sing it.

There came a time when Rama was going to perform a huge sacrifice, or Yajna, such as the old kings used to celebrate. But no ceremony in India can be performed by a married man without his wife: he must have the wife with him, the Sahadharmini, the "co-religionist" – that is the expression for a wife. The Hindu householder has to perform hundreds of ceremonies, but not one can be duly performed according to the Shâstras, if he has not a wife to complement it with her part in it.

Now Rama's wife was not with him then, as she had been banished. So, the people asked him to marry again. But at this request Rama for the first time in his life stood against the people. He said, "This cannot be. My life is Sita's." So, as a substitute, a golden statue of Sita was made, in order that the; ceremony could be accomplished. They arranged even a dramatic entertainment, to enhance the religious feeling in this great festival. Valmiki, the great sage-poet, came with his pupils, Lava and Kusha, the unknown sons of Rama. A stage had been erected and everything was ready for the performance. Rama and his brothers attended with all his nobles and his people – a vast audience. Under the direction of Valmiki, the life of Rama was sung by Lava and Kusha, who fascinated the whole assembly by their charming voice and appearance. Poor Rama was nearly maddened, and when in the drama, the scene of Sita's exile came about, he did not know what to do. Then the sage said to him, "Do not be grieved, for I will show you Sita." Then Sita was brought upon the stage and Rama delighted to see his wife. All of a sudden, the old murmur arose: "The test! The test!"

Poor Sita was so terribly overcome by the repeated cruel slight on her reputation that it was more than she could bear. She appealed to the gods to testify to her innocence, when the Earth opened and Sita exclaimed, "Here is the test", and vanished into the bosom of the Earth. The people were taken aback at this tragic end. And Rama was overwhelmed with grief.

A few days after Sita's disappearance, a messenger came to Rama from the gods, who intimated to him that his mission on earth was finished and he was to return to heaven. These tidings brought to him the recognition of his own real Self. He plunged into the waters of Sarayu, the mighty river that laved his capital, and joined Sita in the other world.

This is the great, ancient epic of India. Rama and Sita are the ideals of the Indian nation. All children, especially girls, worship Sita. The height of a woman's ambition is to be like Sita, the pure, the devoted, the all-suffering! When you study these characters, you can at once find out how different is the ideal in India from that of the West. For the race, Sita stands as the ideal of suffering. The West says, "Do! Show your power by doing." India says, "Show your power by suffering." The West has solved the problem of how much a man can have: India has solved the problem of how little a man can have. The two extremes, you see. Sita is typical of India – the idealised India. The question is not whether she ever lived, whether the story is history or not, we know that the ideal is there. There is no other Paurânika story that has so permeated the whole nation, so entered into its very life, and has so tingled in every drop of blood of the race, as this ideal of Sita. Sita is the name in India for everything that is good, pure and holy – everything that in woman we call womanly. If a priest has to bless a woman he says, "Be Sita!"

If he blesses a child, he says "Be Sita!"

They are all children of Sita, and are struggling to be Sita, the patient, the all-suffering, the ever-faithful, the ever-pure wife. Through all this suffering she experiences, there is not one harsh word against

Rama. She takes it as her own duty, and performs her own part in it. Think of the terrible injustice of her being exiled to the forest! But Sita knows no bitterness. That is, again, the Indian ideal. Says the ancient Buddha, "When a man hurts you, and you turn back to hurt him, that would not cure the first injury; it would only create in the world one more wickedness." Sita was a true Indian by nature; she never returned injury.

Who knows which is the truer ideal? The apparent power and strength, as held in the West, or the fortitude in suffering, of the East?

The West says, "We minimise evil by conquering it." India says, "We destroy evil by suffering, until evil is nothing to us, it becomes positive enjoyment." Well, both are great ideals. Who knows which will survive in the long run? Who knows which attitude will really most benefit humanity? Who knows which will disarm and conquer animality? Will it be suffering, or doing?

In the meantime, let us not try to destroy each other's ideals. We are both intent upon the same work, which is the annihilation of evil. You take up your method; let us take up our method. Let us not destroy the ideal. I do not say to the West, "Take up our method." Certainly not. The goal is the same, but the methods can never be the same. And so, after hearing about the ideals of India, I hope that you will say in the same breath to India, "We know, the goal, the ideal, is all right for us both. You follow your own ideal. You follow your method in your own way, and Godspeed to you!"

My message in life is to ask the East and West not to quarrel over different ideals, but to show them that the goal is the same in both cases, however opposite it may appear. As we wend our way through this mazy vale of life, let us bid each other Godspeed.

❑

The Great Teachers of the World

(Delivered at the Shakespeare Club, Pasadena, California, on February 3, 1900)

The universe, according to the theory of the Hindus, is moving in cycles of wave forms. It rises, reaches its zenith, then falls and remains in the hollow, as it were, for some time, once more to rise, and so on, in wave after wave and fall after fall. What is true of the universe is true of every part of it. The march of human affairs is like that. The history of nations is like that: they rise and they fall; after the rise comes a fall, again out of the fall comes a rise, with greater power. This motion is always going on. In the religious world the same movement exists. In every nation's spiritual life, there is a fall as well as a rise. The nation goes down, and everything seems to go to pieces. Then, again, it gains strength, rises; a huge wave comes, sometimes a tidal wave – and always on the topmost crest of the wave is a shining soul, the Messenger. Creator and created by turns, he is the impetus that makes the wave rise, the nation rise: at the same time, he is created by the same forces which make the wave, acting and interacting by turns. He puts forth his tremendous power upon society; and society makes him what he is. These are the great world-thinkers. These are the Prophets of the world, the Messengers of life, the Incarnations of God.

Man has an idea that there can be only one religion, that there can be only one Prophet, and that there can be only one Incarnation; but that idea is not true. By studying the lives of all these great Messengers, we find that each, as it were, was destined to play a part, and a part only; that the harmony consists in the sum total and not in one note. As in the life of races – no race is born to alone enjoy the world. None dare say no. Each race has a part to play in this divine harmony of nations. Each race has its mission to perform, its duty to fulfil. The sum total is the great harmony.

So, not any one of these Prophets is born to rule the world for ever. None has yet succeeded and none is going to be the ruler for ever. Each only contributes a part; and, as to that part, it is true that in the long run every Prophet will govern the world and its destinies.

Most of us are born believers in a personal religion. We talk of principles, we think of theories, and that is all right; but every thought and every movement, every one of our actions, shows that we can only understand the principle when it comes to us through a person. We can grasp an idea only when it comes to us through a materialised ideal person. We can understand the precept only through the example. Would to God that all of us were so developed that we would not require any example, would not require any person. But that we are not; and, naturally, the vast majority of mankind have put their souls at the feet of these extraordinary personalities, the Prophets, the Incarnations of God – Incarnations worshipped by the Christians, by the Buddhists, and by the Hindus. The Mohammedans from the beginning stood against any such worship. They would have nothing to do with worshipping the Prophets or the Messengers, or paying any homage to them; but, practically, instead of one Prophet, thousands upon thousands of saints are being worshipped. We cannot go against facts! We are bound to worship personalities, and it is good.

Remember that word from your great Prophet to the query: "Lord, show us the Father", "He that hath seen me hath seen the Father." Which of us can imagine anything except that He is a man? We can only see Him in and through humanity. The vibration of light is everywhere in this room: why cannot lie see it everywhere? You have to see it only in that lamp. God is an Omnipresent Principle – everywhere: but we are so constituted at present that we can see Him, feel Him, only in and through a human God. And when these great Lights come, then man realises God. And they come in a different way from what we come. We come as beggars; they come as Emperors. We come here like orphans, as people who have lost their way and do not know it. What are we to do? We do not know what is the meaning of our lives. We cannot realise it. Today we are doing one thing, tomorrow another. We are like little bits of straw rocking to and fro in water, like feathers blown about in a hurricane.

But, in the history of mankind, you will find that there come these Messengers, and that from their very birth their mission is found and formed. The whole plan is there, laid down; and you see them swerving not one inch from that. Because they come with a mission, they come with a message, they do not want to reason. Did you ever hear or read of these great Teachers, or Prophets, reasoning out what they taught? No, not one of them did so. They speak direct. Why should they reason? They see the Truth. And not only do they see it but they show it! If you ask me, "Is there any God ?" and I say "Yes", you immediately ask my grounds for saying so, and poor me has to exercise all his powers to provide you with some reason. If you had come to Christ and said, "Is there any God? " he would have said, "Yes"; and if you had asked, "Is there any proof?" he would have replied, "Behold the Lord!" And thus, you see, it is a direct perception, and not at all the ratiocination of reason. There is no groping in the dark, but there is the strength of direct vision. I see this table; no amount of reason can take that faith from me. It is a direct perception. Such is their faith – faith in their ideals, faith in their mission, faith in themselves, above all else. The great shining Ones believe in themselves as nobody else ever does. The people say, "Do you believe in God? Do you believe in a future life? Do you believe in this doctrine or that dogma?" But here the base is wanting: this belief in oneself. Ay, the man who cannot believe in himself, how can they expect him to believe in anything else? I am not sure of my own existence. One moment I think that I am existing and nothing can destroy me; the next moment I am quaking in fear of death. One minute I think I am immortal; the next minute, a spook appears, and then I don't know what I am, nor where I am. I don't know whether I am living or dead. One moment I think that I am spiritual, that I am moral; and the next moment, a blow comes, and I am thrown flat on my back. And why? – I have lost faith in myself, my moral backbone is broken.

But in these great Teachers you will always find this sign: that they have intense faith in themselves. Such intense faith is unique, and we cannot understand it. That is why we try to explain away in various ways what these Teachers speak of themselves; and people invent twenty thousand theories to explain what they say about their realisation. We do not think of ourselves in the same way, and, naturally, we cannot understand them.

Then again, when they speak, the world is bound to listen. When they speak, each word is direct; it bursts like a bomb-shell. What is in the word, unless it has the Power behind? What matters it what language you speak, and how you arrange your language? What matters it whether you speak correct grammar or with fine rhetoric? What matters it whether your language is ornamental or not? The question is whether or not you have anything to give. It is a question of giving and taking, and not listening. Have you anything to give? – that is the first question. If you have, then give. Words but convey the gift: it is but one of the many modes. Sometimes we do not speak at all. There is an old Sanskrit verse which says, “I saw the Teacher sitting under a tree. He was a young man of sixteen, and the disciple was an old man of eighty. The preaching of the Teacher was silence, and the doubts of the disciple departed."

Sometimes they do not speak at all, but vet they convey the Truth from mind to mind. They come to give. They command, they are the Messengers; you have to receive the Command. Do you not remember in your own scriptures the authority with which Jesus speaks? "Go ye, therefore, and teach all nations . . . teaching them to observe all things whatsoever I have commanded you." It runs through all his utterances, that tremendous faith in his own message. That you find in the life of all these great giants whom the world worships as its Prophets.

These great Teachers are the living Gods on this earth. Whom else should we worship? I try to get an idea of God in my mind, and I find what a false little thing I conceive; it would be a sin to worship that God. I open my eyes and look at the actual life of these great ones of the earth. They are higher than any conception of God that I could ever form. For, what conception of mercy could a man like me form who would go after a man if he steals anything from me and send him to jail? And what can be my highest idea of forgiveness? Nothing beyond myself. Which of you can jump out of your own bodies? Which of you can jump out of your own minds? Not one of you. What idea of divine love can you form except what you actually live? What we have never experienced we can form no idea of. So, all my best attempts at forming an idea of God would fail in every case. And here are plain facts, and not idealism – actual facts of love, of mercy, of purity, of which I can have no conception even. What wonder that I should fall at the feet of these men and worship them as God? And what else can anyone do? I should like to see the man who can do anything else, however much he may talk. Talking is not actuality. Talking about God and the Impersonal, and this and that is all very good; but these man-Gods are the real Gods of all nations and all races. These divine men have been worshipped and will be worshipped so long as man is man. Therein is our faith, therein is our hope, of a reality. Of what avail is a mere mystical principle!

The purpose and intent of what I have to say to you is this, that I have found it possible in my life to worship all of them, and to be ready for all that are yet to come. A mother recognises her son in any dress in which he may appear before her; and if one does not do so, I am sure she is not the mother of that man. Now, as regards those of you that think that you understand Truth and Divinity and God in only one Prophet in the world, and not in any other, naturally, the conclusion which I draw is that you do not understand Divinity in anybody; you have simply swallowed words and identified yourself with one sect, just as you would in party politics, as a matter of opinion; but that is no religion at all. There are some fools in this world who use brackish water although there is excellent sweet water near by, because, they say, the brackish-water well was dug by their father. Now, in my little experience I have collected this knowledge – that for all the devilry that religion is, blamed with, religion is not at all in fault: no religion ever persecuted men, no religion ever burnt witches, no religion ever did any of these things. What then incited people to do these things? Politics, but never religion; and if such politics takes the name of religion whose fault is that?

So, when each man stands and says "My Prophet is the only true Prophet," he is not correct – he knows not the alpha of religion. Religion is neither talk, nor theory, nor intellectual consent. It is realisation in the heart of our hearts; it is touching God; it is feeling, realising that I am a spirit in relation with the Universal Spirit and all Its great manifestations. If you have really entered the house of the Father, how can you have seen His children and not known them? And if you do not recognise them, you have not entered the house of the Father. The mother recognises her child in any dress and knows him however disguised. Recognise all the great, spiritual men and women in every age and country, and see that they are not really at variance with one another. Wherever there has been actual religion – this touch of the Divine, the soul coming in direct sense-contact with the Divine – there has always been a broadening of the mind which enables it to see the light everywhere. Now, some Mohammedans are the crudest in this respect, and the most sectarian. Their watchword is: "There is one God, and Mohammed is His Prophet." Everything beyond that not only is bad, but must be destroyed forthwith; at a moment's notice, every man or woman who does not exactly believe in that must be killed; everything that does not belong to this worship must be immediately broken; every book that teaches any thing else must be burnt. From the Pacific to the Atlantic, for five hundred years blood ran all over the world. That is Mohammedanism! Nevetheless, among these Mohammedans, wherever there has a philosophic man, he was sure to protest against these cruelties. In that he showed the touch of the Divine and realised a fragment of the truth; he was not playing with his religion; for it was not his father's religion he was talking, but spoke the truth direct like a man.

Side by side with tie modern theory of evolution, there is another thing: atavism. There is a tendency in us to revert to old ideas in religion. Let us think something new, even if it be wrong. It is better to do that. Why should you not try to hit the mark? We become wiser through failures. Time is infinite. Look at the wall. Did the wall ever tell a lie? It is always the wall. Man tells a lie – and becomes a god too. It is better to do something; never mind even if it proves to be wrong it is better than doing nothing. The cow never tells a lie, but she remains a cow, all the time. Do something! Think some thought; it doesn't matter whether you are right or wrong. But think something! Because my forefathers did not think this way, shall I sit down quietly and gradually lose my sense of feeling and my own thinking faculties? I may as well be dead! And what is life worth if we have no living ideas, no convictions of our own about religion? There is some hope for the atheists, because though they differ from others, they think for themselves. The people who never think anything for themselves are not yet born into the world of religion; they have a mere jelly-fish existence. They will not think; they do not care for religion. But the disbeliever, the atheist, cares, and he is struggling. So think something! Struggle Godward! Never mind if you fail, never mind if you get hold of a queer theory. If you are afraid to be called queer, keep it in your own mind – you need not go and preach it to others. But do something! Struggle Godward! Light must come. If a man feeds me every day of my life, in the long run I shall lose the use of my hands. Spiritual death is the result of following each other like a flock of sheep. Death is the result of inaction. Be active; and wherever there is activity, there must be difference. Difference is the sauce of life; it is the beauty, it is the art of everything. Difference makes all beautiful here. It is variety that is the source of life, the sign of life. Why should we be afraid of it?

Now, we are coming into a position to understand about the Prophets. Now, we see that the historical evidence is – apart from the jelly-fish existence in religion – that where there has been any real thinking, any real love for God, the soul has grown Godwards and has got as it were, a glimpse now and then, has come into direct perception, even for a second, even once in its life. Immediately, "All doubts vanish for ever, and all the crookedness of the heart is made straight, and all bondages vanish, and the results of action and Karma fly when He is seen who is the nearest of the near and the farthest of the far." That is religion, that is all of religion; the rest is mere theory, dogma, so many ways of going to that state of direct perception. Now we are fighting over the basket and the fruits have fallen into the ditch.

If two men quarrel about religion, just ask them the question: "Have you seen God? Have you seen these things?" One man says that Christ is the only Prophet: well, has he seen Christ? "Has your father seen Him?" "No, Sir." "Has your grandfather seen Him?" "No, Sir." "Have you seen Him?" "No, Sir." "Then what are you quarrelling for? The fruits have fallen into the ditch, and you are quarrelling over the basket!"

Sensible men and women should be ashamed to go on quarrelling in that way!

These great Messengers and Prophets are great and true. Why? Because, each one has come to preach a great idea. Take the Prophets of India, for instance. They are the oldest of the founders of religion. We takes first, Krishna. You who have read the Gitâ see all through the book that the one idea is non-attachment. Remain unattached. The heart's love is due to only One. To whom? To Him who never changeth. Who is that One? It is God. Do not make the mistake of giving the heart to anything that is changing, because that is misery. You may give it to a man; but if he dies, misery is the result. You may give it to a friend, but he may tomorrow become your enemy. If you give it to your husband, he may one day quarrel with you. You may give it to your wife, and she may die the day after tomorrow. Now, this is the way the world is going on. So says Krishna in the Gita: The Lord is the only One who never changes. His love never fails. Wherever we are and whatever we do, He is ever and ever the same merciful, the same loving heart. He never changes, He is never angry, whatever we do. How can God be angry with us? Your babe does many mischievous things: are you angry with that babe? Does not God know what we are going to be? He knows we are all going to be perfect, sooner or later. He has patience, infinite patience. We must love Him, and everyone that lives – only in and through Him. This is the keynote. You must love the wife, but not for the wife's sake. "Never, O Beloved, is the husband loved on account of the husband, but because the Lord is in the husband." The Vedanta philosophy says that even in the love of the husband and wife, although the wife is thinking that she is loving the husband, the real attraction is the Lord, who is present there. He is the only attraction, there is no other; but the wife in most cases does not know that it is so, but ignorantly she is doing the right thing, which is, loving the Lord. Only, when one does it ignorantly, it may bring pain. If one does it knowingly, that is salvation. This is what our scriptures say. Wherever there is love, wherever there is a spark of joy, know that to be a spark of His presence because He is joy, blessedness, and love itself. Without that there cannot be any love.

This is the trend of Krishna's instruction all the time. He has implanted that upon his race, so that when a Hindu does anything, even if he drinks water, he says "If there is virtue in it, let it go to the Lord." The Buddhist says, if he does any good deed, "Let the merit of the good deed belong to the world; if there is any virtue in what I do, let it go to the world, and let the evils of the world come to me." The Hindu says he is a great believer in God; the Hindu says that God is omnipotent and that He is the Soul of every soul everywhere; the Hindu says, If I give all my virtues unto Him, that is the greatest sacrifice, and they will go to the whole universe."

Now, this is one phase; and what is the other message of Krishna? "Whosoever lives in the midst of the world, and works, and gives up all the fruit of his action unto the Lord, he is never touched with the evils of the world. Just as the lotus, born under the water, rises up and blossoms above the water, even so is the man who is engaged in the activities of the world, giving up all the fruit of his activities unto the Lord" (Gita, V. 10).

Krishna strikes another note as a teacher of intense activity. Work, work, work day and night, says the Gita. You may ask, "Then, where is peace? If all through life I am to work like a cart-horse and die in harness, what am I here for?" Krishna says, "Yes, you will find peace. Flying from work is never the way to find peace." Throw off your duties if you can, and go to the top of a mountain; even there the mind is going – whirling, whirling, whirling. Someone asked a Sannyasin, "Sir, have you found a nice place? How many years have you been travelling in the Himalayas?" "For forty years," replied the Sannyasin. "There are many beautiful spots to select from, and to settle down in: why did you not do so?" "Because for these forty years my mind would not allow me to do so." We all say, "Let us find peace"; but the mind will not allow us to do so.

You know the story of the man who caught a Tartar. A soldier was outside the town, and he cried out when be came near the barracks, "I have caught a Tartar." A voice called out, "Bring him in." "He won't come in, sir." "Then you come in." "He won't let me come in, sir." So, in this mind of ours, we have "caught a Tartar": neither can we tone it down, nor will it let us be toned down. We have all "caught Tartars". We all say, be quiet, and peaceful, and so forth. But every baby can say that and thinks he can do it. However, that is very difficult. I have tried. I threw overboard all my duties and fled to the tops of mountains; I lived in caves and deep forests – but all the same, I "caught a Tartar" because I had my world with me all the time. The "Tartar" is what I have in my own mind, so we must not blame poor people outside. "These circumstances are good, and these are bad," so we say, while the "Tartar" is here, within; if we can quiet him down, we shall be all right.

Therefore Krishna teaches us not to shirk our duties, but to take them up manfully, and not think of the result. The servant has no right to question. The soldier has no right to reason. Go forward, and do not pay too much attention to the nature of the work you have to do. Ask your mind if you are unselfish. If you are, never mind anything, nothing can resist you! Plunge in! Do the duty at hand. And when you have done this, by degrees you will realise the Truth: "Whosoever in the midst of intense activity finds intense peace, whosoever in the midst of the greatest peace finds the greatest activity, he is a Yogi, he is a great soul, he has arrived at perfection."

Now, you see that the result of this teaching is that all the duties of the world are sanctified. There is no duty in this world which we have any right to call menial: and each man's work is quite as good as that of the emperor on his throne.

Listen to Buddha's message – a tremendous message. It has a place in our heart. Says Buddha, "Root out selfishness, and everything that makes you selfish. Have neither wife, child, nor family. Be not of the world; become perfectly unselfish." A worldly man thinks he will be unselfish, but when he looks at the face of his wife it makes him selfish. The mother thinks she will be perfectly unselfish, but she looks at her baby, and immediately selfishness comes. So with everything in this world. As soon as selfish desires arise, as soon as some selfish pursuit is followed, immediately the whole man, the real man, is gone: he is like a brute, he is a slave' he forgets his fellow mcn. No more does he say, "You first and I afterwards," but it is "I first and let everyone else look out for himself."

We find that Krishna's message has also a place for us. Without that message, we cannot move at all. We cannot conscientiously and with peace, joy, and happiness, take up any duty of our lives without listening to the message of Krishna: "Be not afraid even if there is evil in your work, for there is no work which has no evil." "Leave it unto the Lord, and do not look for the results."

On the other hand, there is a corner in the heart for the other message: Time flies; this world is finite and all misery. With your good food, nice clothes, and your comfortable home, O sleeping man and woman, do you ever think of the millions that are starving and dying? Think of the great fact that it is all misery, misery, misery! Note the first utterance of the child: when it enters into the world, it weeps. That is the fact – the child-weeps. This is a place for weeping! If we listen to the Messenger, we should not be selfish.

Behold another Messenger, He of Nazareth. He teaches, "Be ready, for the Kingdom of Heaven is at hand." I have pondered over the message of Krishna, and am trying to work without attachment, but sometimes I forget. Then, suddenly, comes to me the message of Buddha: "Take care, for everything in the world as evanescent, and there is always misery in this life." I listen to that, and I am uncertain which to accept. Then again comes, like a thunderbolt, the message: "Be ready, for the Kingdom of Heaven is at hand." Do not delay a moment. Leave nothing for tomorrow. Get ready for the final event, which may overtake you immediately, even now. That message, also, has a place, and we acknowledge it. We salute the Messenger, we salute the Lord.

And then comes Mohammed, the Messenger of equality. You ask, "What good can there be in his religion?" If there were no good, how could it live? The good alone lives, that alone survives; because the good alone is strong, therefore it survives. How long is the life of an impure man, even in this life? Is not the life of the pure man much longer? Without doubt, for purity is strength, goodness is strength. How could Mohammedanism have lived, had there been nothing good in its teaching? There is much good. Mohammed was the Prophet of equality, of the brotherhood of man, the brotherhood of all Mussulmans

So we see that each Prophet, each Messenger, has a particular message. When you first listen to that message, and then look at his life, you see his whole life stands explained, radiant.

Now, ignorant fools start twenty thousand theories, and put forward, according to their own mental development, explanations to suit their own ideas, and ascribe them to these great Teachers. They take their teachings and put their misconstruction upon them. With every great Prophet his life is the only commentary. Look at his life: what he did will bear out the texts. Read the Gita, and you will find that it is exactly borne out by the life of the Teacher.

Mohammed by his life showed that amongst Mohammedans there should be perfect equality and brotherhood. There was no question of race, caste, creed, colour, or sex. The Sultan of Turkey may buy a Negro from the mart of Africa, and bring him in chains to Turkey; but should he become a Mohammedan and have sufficient merit and abilities, he might even marry the daughter of the Sultan. Compare this with the way in which the Negroes and the American Indians are treated in this country! And what do Hindus do? If one of your missionaries chance to touch the food of an orthodox person, he would throw it away. Notwithstanding our grand philosophy, you note our weakness in practice; but there You see the greatness of the Mohammedan beyond other races, showing itself in equality, perfect equality regardless of race or colour.

Will other and greater Prophets come? Certainly they will come in this world. But do not look forward to that. I should better like that each one of you became a Prophet of this real New Testament, which is made up of all the Old Testaments. Take all the old messages, supplement them with your own realisations, and become a Prophet unto others. Each one of these Teachers has been great; each has left something for us; they have been our Gods. We salute them, we are their servants; and, all the same, we salute ourselves; for if they have been Prophets and children of God, we also are the same. They reached their perfection, and we are going to attain ours now. Remember the words of Jesus: "The Kingdom of Heaven is at hand!"

This very moment let everyone of us make a staunch resolution: "I will become a Prophet, I will become a messenger of Light, I will become a child of God, nay, I will become a God!"

❑

Buddha's Message to the World

(Delivered in San Francisco, on March 18, 1900)

Buddhism is historically the most important religion – historically, not philosophically – because it was the most tremendous religious movement that the world ever saw, the most gigantic spiritual wave ever to burst upon human society. There is no civilisation on which its effect has not been felt in some way or other.

The followers of Buddha were most enthusiastic and very missionary in spirit. They were the first among the adherents of various religions not to remain content with the limited sphere of their Mother Church. They spread far and wide. They travelled east and west, north and south. They reached into darkest Tibet; they went into Persia, Asia Minor; they went into Russia, Poland, and many other countries of the Western world. They went into China, Korea, Japan; they went into Burma, Siam, the East Indies, and beyond. When Alexander the Great, through his military conquests, brought the Mediterranean world in contact with India, the wisdom of India at once found a channel through which to spread over vast portions of Asia and Europe. Buddhist priests went out teaching among the different nations; and as they taught, superstition and priestcraft began to vanish like mist before the sun.

To understand this movement properly you should know what conditions prevailed in India at the time Buddha came, just as to understand Christianity you have to grasp the state of Jewish society at the time of Christ. It is necessary that you have an idea of Indian society six hundred years before the birth of Christ, by which time Indian civilisation had already completed its growth.

When you study the civilisation of India, you find that it has died and revived several times; this is its peculiarity. Most races rise once and then decline for ever. There are two kinds of people; those who grow continually and those whose growth comes to an end. The peaceful nations, India and China, fall down, yet rise again; but the others, once they go down, do not come up – they die. Blessed are the peacemakers, for they shall enjoy the earth.

At the time Buddha was born, India was in need of a great spiritual leader, a prophet. There was already a most powerful body of priests. You will understand the situation better if you remember the history of the Jews – how they had two types of religious leaders, priests and prophets, the priests keeping the people in ignorance and grinding superstitions into their minds. The methods of worship the priests prescribed were only a means by which they could dominate the people. All through the Old Testament, you find the prophets challenging the superstitions of the priests. The outcome of this fight was the triumph of the prophets and the defeat of the priests.

Priests believe that there is a God, but that this God can be approached and known only through them. People can enter the Holy of Holies only with the permission of the priests. You must pay them, worship them, place everything in their hands. Throughout the history of the world, this priestly tendency has cropped up again and again – this tremendous thirst for power, this tiger-like thirst, seems a part of human nature. The priests dominate you, lay down a thousand rules for you. They describe simple truths in roundabout ways. They tell you stories to support their own superior position. If you want to thrive in this life or go to heaven after death, you have to pass through their hands. You have to perform all kinds of ceremonies and rituals. All this has made life so complicated and has so confused the brain that if I give you plain words, you will go home unsatisfied. You have become thoroughly befuddled. The less you understand, the better you feel! The prophets have been giving warnings against the priests and their superstitions and machinations; but the vast mass of people have not yet learnt to heed these warnings – education is yet to come to them.

Men must have education. They speak of democracy, of the equality of all men, these days. But how will a man know he is equal with all? He must have a strong brain, a clear mind free of nonsensical ideas; he must pierce through the mass of superstitions encrusting his mind to the pure truth that is in his inmost Self. Then he will know that all perfections, all powers are already within himself, that these have not to be given him by others. When he realises this, he becomes free that moment, he achieves equality. He also realises that every one else is equally as perfect as he, and he does not have to exercise any power, physical, mental or moral, over his brother men. He abandons the idea that there was ever any man who was lower than himself. Then he can talk of equality; not until then.

Now, as I was telling you, among the Jews there was a continuous struggle between the priests and the prophets; and the priests sought to monopolise power and knowledge, till they themselves began to lose them and the chains they had put on the feet of the people were on their own feet. The masters always become slaves before long. The culmination of the struggle was the victory of Jesus of Nazareth. This triumph is the history of Christianity. Christ at last succeeded in overthrowing the mass of witchcraft. This great prophet killed the dragon of priestly selfishness, rescued from its clutches the jewel of truth, and gave it to all the world, so that whosoever desired to possess it would have absolute freedom to do so, and would not have to wait on the pleasure of any priest or priests.

The Jews were never a very philosophical race: they had not the subtlety of the Indian brain nor did they have the Indian's psychic power. The priests in India, the Brahmins, possessed great intellectual and psychic powers. It was they who began the spiritual development of India, and they accomplished wonderful things. But the time came when the free spirit of development that had at first actuated the Brahmins disappeared. They began to arrogate powers and privileges to themselves. If a Brahmin killed a man, he would not be punished. The Brahmin, by his very birth, is the lord of the universe! Even the most wicked Brahmin must be worshipped!

But while the priests were flourishing, there existed also the poet-prophets called Sannyâsins. All Hindus, whatever their castes may be, must, for the sake of attaining spirituality, give up their work and prepare for death. No more is the world to be of any interest to them. They must go out and become Sannyasins. The Sannyasins have nothing to do with the two thousand ceremonies that the priests have invented: Pronounce certain words – ten syllables, twenty syllables, and so on – all these things are nonsense.

So these poet-prophets of ancient India repudiated the ways of the priest and declared the pure truth. They tried to break the power of the priests, and they succeeded a little. But in two generations their disciples went back to the superstitious, roundabout ways of the priests – became priests themselves: "You can get truth only through us!"

Truth became crystallised again, and again prophets came to break the encrustations and free the truth, and so it went on. Yes, there must be all the time the man, the prophet, or else humanity will die.

You wonder why there have to be all these roundabout methods of the priests. Why can you not come directly to the truth? Are you ashamed of God's truth that you have to hide it behind all kinds of intricate ceremonies and formulas? Are you ashamed of God that you cannot confess His truth before the world? Do you call that being religious and spiritual? The priests are the only people fit for the truth! The masses are not fit for it! It must be diluted! Water it down a little!

Take the Sermon on the Mount and the Gitâ – they are simplicity itself. Even the streetwalker can understand them. How grand! In them you find the truth clearly and simply revealed. But no, the priests would not accept that truth can be found so directly. They speak of two thousand heavens and two thousand hells. If people follow their prescriptions, they will go to heaven! If they do not obey the rules, they will go to hell!

But the people shall learn the truth. Some are afraid that if the full truth is given to all, it will hurt them. They should not be given the unqualified truth

– so they say. But the world is not much better off by compromising truth. What worse can it be than it is already? Bring truth out! If it is real, it will do good. When people protest and propose other methods, they only make apologies for witchcraft.

India was full of it in Buddha's day. There were the masses of people, and they were debarred from all knowledge. If just a word of the Vedas entered the ears of a man, terrible punishment was visited upon him. The priests had made a secret of the Vedas – the Vedas that contained the spiritual truths discovered by the ancient Hindus!

At last one man could bear it no more. He had the brain, the power, and the heart – a heart as infinite as the broad sky. He felt how the masses were being led by the priests and how the priests were glorying in their power, and he wanted to do something about it. He did not want any power over any one, and he wanted to break the mental and spiritual bonds of men. His heart was large. The heart, many around us may have, and we also want to help others. But we do not have the brain; we do not know the ways and means by which help can be given. But this man had the brain to discover the means of breaking the bondages of souls. He learnt why men suffer, and he found the way out of suffering. He was a man of accomplishment, he worked everything out; he taught one and all without distinction and made them realise the peace of enlightenment. This was the man Buddha.

You know from Arnold's poem, The Light of Asia, how Buddha was born a prince and how the misery of the world struck him deeply; how, although brought up and living in the lap of luxury, he could not find comfort in his personal happiness and security; how he renounced the world, leaving his princess and new-born son behind; how he wandered searching for truth from teacher to teacher; and how he at last attained to enlightenment. You know about his long mission, his disciples, his organisations. You all know these things.

Buddha was the triumph in the struggle that had been going on between the priests and the prophets in India. One thing can be said for these Indian priests – they were not and never are intolerant of religion; they never have persecuted religion. Any man was allowed to preach against them. Theirs is such a religion; they never molested any one for his religious views. But they suffered from the peculiar weaknesses of all the priests: they also sought power, they also promulgated rules and regulations and made religion unnecessarily complicated, and thereby undermined the strength of those who followed their religion.

Buddha cut through all these excrescences. He preached the most tremendous truths. He taught the very gist of the philosophy of the Vedas to one and all without distinction, he taught it to the world at large, because one of his great messages was the equality of man. Men are all equal. No concession there to anybody! Buddha was the great preacher of equality. Every man and woman has the same right to attain spirituality – that was his teaching. The difference between the priests and the other castes he abolished. Even the lowest were entitled to the highest attainments; he opened the door of Nirvâna to one and all. His teaching was bold even for India. No amount of preaching can ever shock the Indian soul, but it was hard for India to swallow Buddha's doctrine. How much harder it must be for you!

His doctrine was this: Why is there misery in our life? Because we are selfish. We desire things for ourselves – that is why there is misery. What is the way out? The giving up of the self. The self does not exist; the phenomenal world, all this that we perceive, is all that exists. There is nothing called soul underlying the cycle of life and death. There is the stream of thought, one thought following another in succession, each thought coming into existence and becoming non-existent at the same moment, that is all; there is no thinker of the thought, no soul. The body is changing all the time; so is mind, consciousness. The self therefore is a delusion. All selfishness comes of holding on to the self, to this illusory self. If we know the truth that there is no self, then we will be happy and make others happy.

This was what Buddha taught. And he did not merely talk; he was ready to give up his own life for the world. He said, "If sacrificing an animal is good, sacrificing a man is better", and he offered himself as a sacrifice. He said, "This animal sacrifice is another superstition. God and soul are the two big superstitions. God is only a superstition invented by the priests. If there is a God, as these Brahmins preach, why is there so much misery in the world? He is just like me, a slave to the law of causation. If he is not bound by the law of causation, then why does he create? Such a God is not at all satisfactory. There is the ruler in heaven that rules the universe according to his sweet will and leaves us all here to die in misery – he never has the goodness to look at us for a moment. Our whole life is continuous suffering; but this is not sufficient punishment – after death we must go to places where we have other punishments. Yet we continually perform all kinds of rites and ceremonies to please this creator of the world!"

Buddha said, "These ceremonials are all wrong. There is but one ideal in the world. Destroy all delusions; what is true will remain. As soon as the clouds are gone, the sun will shine". How to kill the self? Become perfectly unselfish, ready to give up your life even for an ant. Work not for any superstition, not to please any God, not to get any reward, but because you are seeking your own release by killing your self. Worship and prayer and all that, these are all nonsense. You all say, "I thank God" – but where does He live? You do not know, and yet you are all going crazy about God.

Hindus can give up everything except their God. To deny God is to cut off the very ground from under the feet of devotion. Devotion and God the Hindus must cling to. They can never relinquish these. And here, in the teaching of Buddha, are no God and no soul – simply work. What for? Not for the self, for the self is a delusion. We shall be ourselves when this delusion has vanished. Very few are there in the world that can rise to that height and work for work's sake.

Yet the religion of Buddha spread fast. It was because of the marvellous love which, for the first time in the history of humanity, overflowed a large heart and devoted itself to the service not only of all men but of all living things – a love which did not care for anything except to find a way of release from suffering for all beings.

Man was loving God and had forgotten all about his brother man. The man who in the name of God can give up his very life, can also turn around and kill his brother man in the name of God. That was the state of the world. They would sacrifice the son for the glory of God, would rob nations for the glory of God, would kill thousands of beings for the glory of God, would drench the earth with blood for the glory of God. This was the first time they turned to the other God – man. It is man that is to be loved. It was the first wave of intense love for all men – the first wave of true unadulterated wisdom – that, starting from India, gradually inundated country after country, north, south, east, west.

This teacher wanted to make truth shine as truth. No softening, no compromise, no pandering to the priests, the powerful, the kings. No bowing before superstitious traditions, however hoary; no respect for forms and books just because they came down from the distant past. He rejected all scriptures, all forms of religious practice. Even the very language, Sanskrit, in which religion had been traditionally taught in India, he rejected, so that his followers would not have any chance to imbibe the superstitions which were associated with it.

There is another way of looking at the truth we have been discussing: the Hindu way. We claim that Buddha's great doctrine of selflessness can be better understood if it is looked at in our way. In the Upanishads there is already the great doctrine of the Âtman and the Brahman. The Atman, Self, is the same as Brahman, the Lord. This Self is all that is; It is the only reality. Mâyâ, delusion, makes us see It as different. There is one Self, not many. That one Self shines in various forms. Man is man's brother because all men are one. A man is not only my brother, say the Vedas, he is myself. Hurting any part of the universe, I only hurt myself. I am the universe. It is a delusion that I think I am Mr. So-and-so – that is the delusion.

Thc morc you approach your real Self, the more this delusion vanishes. The more all differences and divisions disappear, the more you realise all as the one Divinity. God exists; but He is not the man sitting upon a cloud. He is pure Spirit. Where does He reside? Nearer to you than your very self. He is the Soul. How can you perceive God as separate and different from yourself? When you think of Him as some one separate from yourself, you do not know Him. He is you yourself. That was the doctrine of the prophets of India.

It is selfishness that you think that you see Mr. So-and-so and that all the world is different from you. You believe you are different from me. You do not take any thought of me. You go home and have your dinner and sleep. If I die, you still eat, drink, and are merry. But you cannot really be happy when the rest of the world is suffering. We are all one. It is the delusion of separateness that is the root of misery. Nothing exists but the Self; there is nothing else.

Buddha's idea is that there is no God, only man himself. He repudiated the mentality which underlies the prevalent ideas of God. He found it made men weak and superstitious. If you pray to God to give you everything, who is it, then, that goes out and works? God comes to those who work hard. God helps them that help themselves. An opposite idea of God weakens our nerves, softens our muscles, makes us dependent. Everything independent is happy; everything dependent is miserable. Man has infinite power within himself, and he can realise it – he can realise himself as the one infinite Self. It can be done; but you do not believe it. You pray to God and keep your powder dry all the time.

Buddha taught the opposite. Do not let men weep. Let them have none of this praying and all that. God is not keeping shop. With every breath you are praying in God. I am talking; that is a prayer. You are listening; that is a prayer. Is there ever any movement of yours, mental or physical, in which you do not participate in the infinite Divine Energy? It is all a constant prayer. If you call only a set of words prayer, you make prayer superficial. Such prayers are not much good; they can scarcely bear any real fruit.

Is prayer a magic formula, by repeating which, even is you do not work hard, you gain miraculous results? No. All have to work hard; all have to reach the depths of that infinite Energy. Behind the poor, behind the rich, there is the same infinite Energy. It is not that one man works hard, and another by repeating a few words achieves results. This universe is a constant prayer. If you take prayer in this sense, I am with you. Words are not necessary. Better is silent prayer.

The vast majority of people do not understand the meaning of this doctrine. In India any compromise regarding the Self means that we have given power into the hands of the priests and have forgotten the great teachings of the prophets. Buddha knew this; so he brushed aside all the priestly doctrines and practices and made man stand on his own feet. It was necessary for him to go against the accustomed ways of the people; he had to bring about revolutionary changes. As a result this sacrificial religion passed away from India for ever, and was never revived.

Buddhism apparently has passed away from India; but really it has not. There was an element of danger in the teaching of Buddha – it was a reforming religion. In order to bring about the tremendous spiritual change he did, he had to give many negative teachings. But if a religion emphasises the negative side too much, it is in danger of eventual destruction. Never can a reforming sect survive if it is only reforming; the formative elements alone – the real impulse, that is, the principles – live on and on. After a reform has been brought about, it is the positive side that should be emphasised; after the building is finished the scaffolding must be taken away.

It so happened in India that as time went on, the followers of Buddha emphasised the negative aspect of his teachings too much and thereby caused the eventual downfall of their religion. The positive aspects of truth were suffocated by the forces of negation; and thus India repudiated the destructive tendencies that flourished in the name of Buddhism. That was the decree of the Indian national thought.

The negative elements of Buddhism – there is no God and no soul —died out. I can say that God is the only being that exists; it is a very positive statement. He is the one reality. When Buddha says there is no soul, I say, "Man, thou art one with the universe; thou art all things." How positive! The reformative element died out; but the formative element has lived through all time. Buddha taught kindness towards lower beings; and since then there has not been a sect in India that has not taught charity to all beings, even to animals. This kindness, this mercy, this charity – greater than any doctrine – are what Buddhism left to us.

The life of Buddha has an especial appeal. All my life I have been very fond of Buddha, but not of his doctrine. I have more veneration for that character than for any other – that boldness, that fearlessness, and that tremendous love! He was born for the good of men. Others may seek God, others may seek truth for themselves; he did not even care to know truth for himself. He sought truth because people were in misery. How to help them, that was his only concern. Throughout his life he never had a thought for himself. How can we ignorant, selfish, narrow-minded human beings ever understand the greatness of this man?

And consider his marvellous brain! No emotionalism. That giant brain never was superstitious. Believe not because an old manuscript has been produced, because it has been handed down to you from your forefathers, because your friends want you to – but think for yourself; search truth for yourself; realise it yourself. Then if you find it beneficial to one and many, give it to people. Soft-brained men, weak-minded, chicken-hearted, cannot find the truth. One has to be free, and as broad as the sky. One has to have a mind that is crystal clear; only then can truth shine in it. We are so full of superstitions! Even in your country where you think you are highly educated, how full of narrownesses and superstitions you are! Just think, with all your claims to civilisation in this country, on one occasion I was refused a chair to sit on, because I was a Hindu.

Six hundred years before the birth of Christ, at the time when Buddha lived, the people of India must have had wonderful education. Extremely free-minded they must have been. Great masses followed him. Kings gave up their thrones; queens gave up their thrones. People were able to appreciate and embrace his teaching, so revolutionary, so different from what they had been taught by the priests through the ages! But their minds have been unusually free and broad.

And consider his death. If he was great in life, he was also great in death. He ate food offered to him by a member of a race similar to your American Indians. Hindus do not touch them, because they eat everything indiscriminately. He told his disciples, "Do not eat this food, but I cannot refuse it. Go to the man and tell him he has done me one of the greatest services of my life – he has released me from the body." An old man came and sat near him – he had walked miles and miles to see the Master – and Buddha taught him. When he found a disciple weeping, he reproved him, saying, "What is this? Is this the result of all my teaching? Let there be no false bondage, no dependence on me, no false glorification of this passing personality. The Buddha is not a person; he is a realisation. Work out your own salvation."

Even when dying, he would not claim any distinction for himself. I worship him for that. What you call Buddhas and Christs are only the names of certain states of realisation. Of all the teachers of the world, he was the one who taught us most to be self-reliant, who freed us not only from the bondages of our false selves but from dependence on the invisible being or beings called God or gods. He invited every one to enter into that state of freedom which he called Nirvana. All must attain to it one day; and that attainment is the complete fulfilment of man.

❑

My Life and Mission

(Delivered at the Shakespeare Club House, in Pasadena, California, on January 27, 1900)

Now, ladies and gentlemen, the subject for this morning was to have been the Vedanta Philosophy. That subject itself is interesting, but rather dry and very vast.

Meanwhile, I have been asked by your president and some of the ladies and gentlemen here to tell them something about my work and what I have been doing. It may be interesting to some here, but not so much so to me. In fact, I do not quite know how to tell it to you, for this will have been the first time in my life that I have spoken on that subject.

Now, to understand what I have been trying to do, in my small way, I will take you, in imagination, to India. We have not time to go into all the details and all the ramifications of the subject; nor is it possible for you to understand all the complexities in a foreign race in this short time. Suffice it to say, I will at least try to give you a little picture of what India is like.

It is like a gigantic building all tumbled down in ruins. At first sight, then, there is little hope. It is a nation gone and ruined. But you wait and study, then you see something beyond that. The truth is that so long as the principle, the ideal, of which the outer man is the expression, is not hurt or destroyed, the man lives, and there is hope for that man. If your coat is stolen twenty times, that is no reason why you should be destroyed. You can get a new coat. The coat is unessential. The fact that a rich man is robbed does not hurt the vitality of the man, does not mean death. The man will survive.

Standing on this principle, we look in and we see – what? India is no longer a political power; it is an enslaved race. Indians have no say, no voice in their own government; they are three hundred millions of slaves – nothing more! The average income of a man in India is two shillings a month. The common state of the vast mass of the people is starvation, so that, with the least decrease in income, millions die. A little famine means death. So there, too, when I look on that side of India, I see ruin-hopeless ruin.

But we find that the Indian race never stood for wealth. Although they acquired immense wealth, perhaps more than any other nation ever acquired, yet the nation did not stand for wealth. It was a powerful race for ages, yet we find that that nation never stood for power, never went out of the country to conquer. Quite content within their own boundaries, they never fought anybody. The Indian nation never stood for imperial glory. Wealth and power, then, were not the ideals of the race.

What then? Whether they were wrong or right – that is not the question we discuss – that nation, among all the children of men, has believed, and believed intensely, that this life is not real. The real is God; and they must cling unto that God through thick and thin. In the midst of their degradation, religion came first. The Hindu man drinks religiously, sleeps religiously, walks religiously, marries religiously, robs religiously.

Did you ever see such a country? If you want to get up a gang of robbers, the leader will have to preach some sort of religion, then formulate some bogus metaphysics, and say that this method is the clearest and quickest way to get God. Then he finds a following, otherwise not. That shows that the vitality of the race, the mission of the race is religion; and because that has not been touched, therefore that race lives.

See Rome. Rome's mission was imperial power, expansion. And so soon as that was touched, Rome fell to pieces, passed out. The mission of Greece was intellect, as soon as that was touched, why, Greece passed out. So in modern times, Spain and all these modern countries. Each nation has a mission for the world. So long as that mission is not hurt, that nation lives, despite every difficulty. But as soon as its mission is destroyed, the nation collapses.

Now, that vitality of India has not been touched yet. They have not given up that, and it is still strong – in spite of all their superstitions. Hideous superstitions are there, most revolting some of them. Never mind. The national life – current is still there – the mission of the race.

The Indian nation never will be a powerful conquering people – never. They will never be a great political power; that is not their business, that is not the note India has to play in the great harmony of nations. But what has she to play? God, and God alone. She clings unto that like grim death. Still there is hope there.

So, then, after your analysis, you come to the conclusion that all these things, all this poverty and misery, are of no consequence – the man is living still, and therefore there is hope.

Well! You see religious activities going on all through the country. I do not recall a year that has not given birth to several new sects in India. The stronger the current, the more the whirlpools and eddies. Sects are not signs of decay, they are a sign of life. Let sects multiply, till the time comes when every one of us is a sect, each individual. We need not quarrel about that.

Now, take your country. (I do not mean any criticism). Here the social laws, the political formation – everything is made to facilitate man's journey in this life. He may live very happily so long as he is on this earth. Look at your streets – how clean! Your beautiful cities! And in how many ways a man can make money! How many channels to get enjoyment in this life! But, if a man here should say, "Now look here, I shall sit down under this tree and meditate; I do not want to work", why, he would have to go to jail. See! There would be no chance for him at all. None. A man can live in this society only if he falls in line. He has to join in this rush for the enjoyment of good in this life, or he dies.

Now let us go back to India. There, if a man says, "I shall go and sit on the top of that mountain and look at the tip of my nose all the rest of my days", everybody says, "Go, and Godspeed to you!"

He need not speak a word. Somebody brings him a little cloth, and he is all right. But if a man says, "Behold, I am going to enjoy a little of this life", every door is closed to him.

I say that the ideas of both countries are unjust. I see no reason why a man here should not sit down and look at the tip of his nose if he likes. Why should everybody here do just what the majority does? I see no reason.

Nor why, in India, a man should not have the goods of this life and make money. But you see how those vast millions are forced to accept the opposite point of view by tyranny. This is the tyranny of the sages. This is the tyranny of the great, tyranny of the spiritual, tyranny of the intellectual, tyranny of the wise. And the tyranny of the wise, mind you, is much more powerful than the tyranny of the ignorant. The wise, the intellectual, when they take to forcing their opinions upon others, know a hundred thousand ways to make bonds and barriers which it is not in the power of the ignorant to break.

Now, I say that this thing has got to stop. There is no use in sacrificing millions and millions of people to produce one spiritual giant. If it is possible to make a society where the spiritual giant will be produced and all the rest of the people will be happy as well, that is good; but if the millions have to be ground down, that is unjust. Better that the one great man should suffer for the salvation of the world.

In every nation you will have to work through their methods. To every man you will have to speak in his own language. Now, in England or in America, if you want to preach religion to them, you will have to work through political methods – make organisations, societies, with voting, balloting, a president, and so on, because that is the language, the method of the Western race. On the other hand, if you want to speak of politics in India, you must speak through the language of religion. You will have to tell them something like this: "The man who cleans his house every morning will acquire such and such an amount of merit, he will go to heaven, or he comes to God." Unless you put it that way, they will not listen to you. It is a question of language.

The thing done is the same. But with every race, you will have to speak their language in order to reach their hearts. And that is quite just. We need not fret about that.

In the Order to which I belong we are called Sannyâsins. The word means "a man who has renounced". This is a very, very, very ancient Order. Even Buddha, who was 560 years before Christ, belonged to that Order. He was one of the reformers of his Order. That was all. So ancient! You find it mentioned away back in the Vedas, the oldest book in the world. In old India there was the regulation that every man and woman, towards the end of their lives, must get out of social life altogether and think of nothing except God and their own salvation. This was to get ready for the great event – death. So old people used to become Sannyasins in those early days. Later on, young people began to give up the world. And young people are active. They could not sit down under a tree and think all the time of their own death, so they went about preaching and starting sects, and so on. Thus, Buddha, being young, started that great reform. Had he been an old man, he would have looked at the tip of his nose and died quietly.

The Order is not a church, and the people who join the Order are not priests. There is an absolute difference between the priests and the Sannyasins. In India, priesthood, like every other business in a social life, is a hereditary profession. A priest's son will become a priest, just as a carpenter's son will be a carpenter, or a blacksmith's son a blacksmith. The priest must always be married. The Hindu does not think a man is complete unless he has a wife. An unmarried man has no right to perform religious ceremonies.

The Sannyasins do not possess property, and they do not marry. Beyond that there is no organisation. The only bond that is there is the bond between the teacher and the taught – and that is peculiar to India. The teacher is not a man who comes just to teach me, and I pay him so much, and there it ends. In India it is really like an adoption. The teacher is more than my own father, and I am truly his child, his son in every respect. I owe him obedience and reverence first, before my own father even; because, they say, the father gave me this body, but he showed me the way to salvation, he is greater than father. And we carry this love, this respect for our teacher all our lives. And that is the only organisation that exists. I adopt my disciples. Sometimes the teacher will be a young man and the disciple a very old man. But never mind, he is the son, and he calls me "Father", and I have to address him as my son, my daughter, and so on.

Now, I happened to get an old man to teach me, and he was very peculiar. He did not go much for intellectual scholarship, scarcely studied books; but when he was a boy he was seized with the tremendous idea of getting truth direct. First he tried by studying his own religion. Then he got the idea that he must get the truth of other religions; and with that idea he joined all the sects, one after another. For the time being he did exactly what they told him to do – lived with the devotees of these different sects in turn, until interpenetrated with the particular ideal of that sect. After a few years he would go to another sect. When he had gone through with all that, he came to the conclusion that they were all good. He had no criticism to offer to any one; they are all so many paths leading to the same goal. And then he said, "That is a glorious thing, that there should be so many paths, because if there were only one path, perhaps it would suit only an individual man. The more the number of paths, the more the chance for every one of us to know the truth. If I cannot be taught in one language, I will try another, and so on". Thus his benediction was for every religion.

Now, all the ideas that I preach are only an attempt to echo his ideas. Nothing is mine originally except the wicked ones, everything I say which is false and wicked. But every word that I have ever uttered which is true and good is simply an attempt to echo his voice. Read his life by Prof. Max Muller. (Ramakrishna: His Life and Sayings, first published in London in 1896. Reprinted in 1951 by Advaita Ashrama.)

Well, there at his feet I conceived these ideas – there with some other young men. I was just a boy. I went there when I was about sixteen. Some of the other boys were still younger, some a little older – about a dozen or more. And together we conceived that this ideal had to be spread. And not only spread, but made practical. That is to say, we must show the spirituality of the Hindus, the mercifulness of the Buddhists, the activity of the Christians, the brotherhood of the Mohammedans, by our practical lives. "We shall start a universal religion now and here," we said, "we will not wait".

Our teacher was an old man who would never touch a coin with his hands. He took just the little food offered, just so many yards of cotton cloth, no more. He could never be induced to take any other gift. With all these marvellous ideas, he was strict, because that made him free. The monk in India is the friend of the prince today, dines with him;

and tomorrow he is with the beggar, sleeps under a tree. He must come into contact with everyone, must always move about. As the saying is, "The rolling stone gathers no moss". The last fourteen years of my life, I have never been for three months at a time in any one place – continually rolling. So do we all.

Now, this handful of boys got hold of these ideas, and all the practical results that sprang out of these ideas. Universal religion, great sympathy for the poor, and all that are very good in theory, but one must practise.

Then came the sad day when our old teacher died. We nursed him the best we could. We had no friends. Who would listen to a few boys, with their crank notions? Nobody. At least, in India, boys are nobodies. Just think of it – a dozen boys, telling people vast, big ideas, saying they are determined to work these ideas out in life. Why, everybody laughed. From laughter it became serious; it became persecution. Why, the parents of the boys came to feel like spanking every one of us. And the more we were derided, the more determined we became.

Then came a terrible time – for me personally and for all the other boys as well. But to me came such misfortune! On the one side was my mother, my brothers. My father died at that time, and we were left poor. Oh, very poor, almost starving all the time! I was the only hope of the family, the only one who could do anything to help them. I had to stand between my two worlds. On the one hand, I would have to see my mother and brothers starve unto death; on the other, I had believed that this man's ideas were for the good of India and the world, and had to be preached and worked out. And so the fight went on in my mind for days and months. Sometimes I would pray for five or six days and nights together without stopping. Oh, the agony of those days! I was living in hell! The natural affections of my boy's heart drawing me to my family – I could not bear to see those who were the nearest and dearest to me suffering. On the other hand, nobody to sympathise with me. Who would sympathise with the imaginations of a boy – imaginations that caused so much suffering to others? Who would sympathise with me? None – except one.

That one's sympathy brought blessing and hope. She was a woman. Our teacher, this great monk, was married when he was a boy and she a mere child. When he became a young man, and all this religious zeal was upon him, she came to see him. Although they had been married for long, they had not seen very much of each other until they were grown up. Then he said to his wife, "Behold, I am your husband; you have a right to this body. But I cannot live the sex life, although I have married you. I leave it to your judgment". And she wept and said, "God speed you! The Lord bless you! Am I the woman to degrade you? If I can, I will help you. Go on in your work".

That was the woman. The husband went on and became a monk in his own way; and from a distance the wife went on helping as much as she could. And later, when the man had become a great spiritual giant, she came – really, she was the first disciple – and she spent the rest of her life taking care of the body of this man. He never knew whether he was living or dying, or anything. Sometimes, when talking, he would get so excited that if he sat on live charcoals, he did not know it. Live charcoals! Forgetting all about his body, all the time.

Well, that lady, his wife, was the only one who sympathised with the idea of those boys. But she was powerless. She was poorer than we were. Never mind! We plunged into the breach. I believed, as I was living, that these ideas were going to rationalise India and bring better days to many lands and foreign races. With that belief, came the realisation that it is better that a few persons suffer than that such ideas should die out of the world. What if a mother or two brothers die? It is a sacrifice. Let it be done. No great thing can be done without sacrifice. The heart must be plucked out and the bleeding heart placed upon the altar. Then great things are done. Is there any other way? None have found it. I appeal to each one of you, to those who have accomplished any great thing. Oh, how much it has cost! What agony! What torture! What terrible suffering is behind every deed of success in every life! You know that, all of you.

And thus we went on, that band of boys. The only thing we got from those around us was a kick and a curse – that was all. Of course, we had to beg from door to door for our food: got hips and haws – the refuse of everything – a piece of bread here and there. We got hold of a broken-down old house, with hissing cobras living underneath; and because that was the cheapest, we went into that house and lived there.

Thus we went on for some years, in the meanwhile making excursions all over India, trying to bring about the idea gradually. Ten years were spent without a ray of light! Ten more years! A thousand times despondency came; but there was one thing always to keep us hopeful – the tremendous faithfulness to each other, the tremendous love between us. I have got a hundred men and women around me; if I become the devil himself tomorrow, they will say, "Here we are still! We will never give you up!"

That is a great blessing. In happiness, in misery, in famine, in pain, in the grave, in heaven, or in hell who never gives me up is my friend. Is such friendship a joke? A man may have salvation through such friendship. That brings salvation if we can love like that. If we have that faithfulness, why, there is the essence of all concentration. You need not worship any gods in the world if you have that faith, that strength, that love. And that was there with us all throughout that hard time. That was there. That made us go from the Himalayas to Cape Comorin, from the Indus to the Brahmaputra.

This band of boys began to travel about. Gradually we began to draw attention: ninety per cent was antagonism, very little of it was helpful. For we had one fault: we were boys – in poverty and with all the roughness of boys. He who has to make his own way in life is a bit rough, he has not much time to be smooth and suave and polite – "my lady and my gentleman", and all that. You have seen that in life, always. He is a rough diamond, he has not much polish, he is a jewel in an indifferent casket.

And there we were. "No compromise!"

was the watchword. "This is the ideal, and this has got to be carried out. If we meet the king, though we die, we must give him a bit of our minds; if the peasant, the same". Naturally, we met with antagonism.

But, mind you, this is life's experience; if you really want the good of others, the whole universe may stand against you and cannot hurt you. It must crumble before your power of the Lord Himself in you if you are sincere and really unselfish. And those boys were that. They came as children, pure and fresh from the hands of nature. Said our Master: I want to offer at the altar of the Lord only those flowers that have not even been smelled, fruits that have not been touched with the fingers. The words of the great man sustained us all. For he saw through the future life of those boys that he collected from the streets of Calcutta, so to say. People used to laugh at him when he said, "You will see – this boy, that boy, what he becomes". His faith was unalterable: "Mother showed it to me. I may be weak, but when She says this is so – She can never make mistakes – it must be so.

"So things went on and on for ten years without any light, but with my health breaking all the time.

It tells on the body in the long run: sometimes one meal at nine in the evening, another time a meal at eight in the morning, another after two days, another after three days – and always the poorest and roughest thing. Who is going to give to the beggar the good things he has? And then, they have not much in India. And most of the time walking, climbing snow peaks, sometimes ten miles of hard mountain climbing, just to get a meal. They eat unleavened bread in India, and sometimes they have it stored away for twenty or thirty days, until it is harder than bricks; and then they will give a square of that. I would have to go from house to house to collect sufficient for one meal. And then the bread was so hard, it made my mouth bleed to eat it. Literally, you can break your teeth on that bread. Then I would put it in a pot and pour over it water from the river. For months and months I existed that way – of course it was telling on the health.

Then I thought, I have tried India: it is time for me to try another country. At that time your Parliament of Religions was to be held, and someone was to be sent from India. I was just a vagabond, but I said, "If you send me, I am going. I have not much to lose, and I do not care if I lose that." It was very difficult to find the money, but after a long struggle they got together just enough to pay for my passage – and

I came. Came one or two months earlier, so that I found myself drifting about in the streets here, without knowing anybody.

But finally the Parliament of Religions opened, and I met kind friends, who helped me right along. I worked a little, collected funds, started two papers, and so on. After that I went over to England and worked there. At the same time I carried on the work for India in America too.

My plan for India, as it has been developed and centralised, is this: I have told you of our lives as monks there, how we go from door to door, so that religion is brought to everybody without charge, except, perhaps, a broken piece of bread. That is why you see the lowest of the low in India holding the most exalted religious ideas. It is all through the work of these monks. But ask a man, "Who are the English?" – he does not know. He says perhaps, "They are the children of those giants they speak of in those books, are they not?" "Who governs you?" "We do not know." "What is the government?" They do not know. But they know philosophy. It is a practical want of intellectual education about life on this earth they suffer from. These millions and millions of people are ready for life beyond this world – is not that enough for them? Certainly not. They must have a better piece of bread and a better piece of rag on their bodies. The great question is: How to get that better bread and better rag for these sunken millions.

First, I must tell you, there is great hope for them, because, you see, they are the gentlest people on earth. Not that they are timid. When they want to fight, they fight like demons. The best soldiers the English have are recruited from the peasantry of India. Death is a thing of no importance to them. Their attitude is "Twenty times I have died before, and I shall die many times after this. What of that?" They never turn back. They are not given to much emotion, but they make very good fighters.

Their instinct, however, is to plough. If you rob them, murder them, tax them, do anything to them, they will be quiet and gentle, so long as you leave them free to practise their religion. They never interfere with the religion of others. "Leave us liberty to worship our gods, and take everything else!"

That is their attitude. When the English touch them there, trouble starts. That was the real cause of the 1857 Mutiny – they would not bear religious repression. The great Mohammedan governments were simply blown up because they touched the Indians' religion.

But aside from that, they are very peaceful, very quiet, very gentle, and, above all, not given to vice. The absence of any strong drink, oh, it makes them infinitely superior to the mobs of any other country. You cannot compare the decency of life among the poor in India with life in the slums here. A slum means poverty, but poverty does not mean sin, indecency, and vice in India. In other countries, the opportunities are such that only the indecent and the lazy need be poor. There is no reason for poverty unless one is a fool or a blackguard – the sort who want city life and all its luxuries. They will not go into the country. They say, "We are here with all the fun, and you must give us bread". But that is not the case in India, where the poor fellows work hard from morning to sunset, and somebody else takes the bread out of their hands, and their children go hungry. Notwithstanding the millions of tons of wheat raised in India, scarcely a grain passes the mouth of a peasant. He lives upon the poorest corn, which you would not feed to your canary-birds.

Now there is no reason why they should suffer such distress – these people; oh, so pure and good! We hear so much talk about the sunken millions and the degraded women of India – but none come to our help. What do they say? They say, "You can only be helped, you can only be good by ceasing to be what you are. It is useless to help Hindus." These people do not know the history of races. There will be no more India if they change their religion and their institutions, because that is the vitality of that race. It will disappear; so, really, you will have nobody to help.

Then there is the other great point to learn: that you can never help really. What can we do for each other? You are growing in your own life, I am growing in my own. It is possible that I can give you a push in your life, knowing that, in the long run, all roads lead to Rome. It is a steady growth. No national civilisation is perfect yet. Give that civilisation a push, and it will arrive at its own goal: do not strive to change it. Take away a nation's institutions, customs, and manners, and what will be left? They hold the nation together.

But here comes the very learned foreign man, and he says, "Look here; you give up all those institutions and customs of thousands of years, and take my tomfool tinpot and be happy". This is all nonsense.

We will have to help each other, but we have to go one step farther: the first thing is to become unselfish in help. "If you do just what I tell you to do, I will help you; otherwise not." Is that help?

And so, if the Hindus want to help you spiritually, there will be no question of limitations: perfect unselfishness. I give, and there it ends. It is gone from me. My mind, my powers, my everything that I have to give, is given: given with the idea to give, and no more. I have seen many times people who have robbed half the world, and they gave $20,000 "to convert the heathen". What for? For the benefit of the heathen, or for their own souls? Just think of that.

And the Nemesis of crime is working. We men try to hoodwink our own eyes. But inside the heart, He has remained, the real Self. He never forgets. We can never delude Him. His eyes will never be hoodwinked. Whenever there is any impulse of real charity, it tells, though it be at the end of a thousand years. Obstructed, it yet wakens once more to burst like a thunderbolt. And every impulse where the motive is selfish, self-seeking – though it may be launched forth with all the newspapers blazoning, all the mobs standing and cheering – it fails to reach the mark.

I am not taking pride in this. But, mark you, I have told the story of that group of boys. Today there is not a village, not a man, not a woman in India that does not know their work and bless them. There is not a famine in the land where these boys do not plunge in and try to work and rescue as many as they can. And that strikes to the heart. The people come to know it. So help whenever you can, but mind what your motive is. If it is selfish, it will neither benefit those you help, nor yourself. If it is unselfish, it will bring blessings upon them to whom it is given, and infinite blessings upon you, sure as you are living. The Lord can never be hoodwinked. The law of Karma can never be hoodwinked.

Well then, my plans are, therefore, to reach these masses of India. Suppose you start schools all over India for the poor, still you cannot educate them. How can you? The boy of four years would better go to the plough or to work, than to your school. He cannot go to your school. It is impossible. Self-preservation is the first instinct. But if the mountain does not go to Mohammed, then Mohammed can come to the mountain. Why should not education go from door to door, say I. If a ploughman's boy cannot come to education, why not meet him at the plough, at the factory, just wherever he is? Go along with him, like his shadow. But there are these hundreds and thousands of monks, educating the people on the spiritual plane; why not let these men do the same work on the intellectual plane? Why should they not talk to the masses a little about history –

about many things? The ears are the best educators. The best principles in our lives were those which we heard from our mothers through our ears. Books came much later. Book-learning is nothing. Through the ears we get the best formative principles. Then, as they get more and more interested, they may come to your books too. First, let it roll on and on – that is my idea.

Well, I must tell you that I am not a very great believer in monastic systems. They have great merits, and also great defects. There should be a perfect balance between the monastics and the householders. But monasticism has absorbed all the power in India. We represent the greatest power. The monk is greater than the prince. There is no reigning sovereign in India who dares to sit down when the "yellow cloth" is there. He gives up his seat and stands. Now, that is bad, so much power, even in the hands of good men – although these monastics have been the bulwark of the people. They stand between the priestcraft and knowledge. They are the centres of knowledge and reform. They are just what the prophets were among the Jews. The prophets were always preaching against the priests, trying to throw out superstitions. So are they in India. But all the same so much power is not good there; better methods should be worked out. But you can only work in the line of least resistance. The whole national soul there is upon monasticism. You go to India and preach any religion as a householder: the Hindu people will turn back and go out. If you have given up the world, however, they say, "He is good, he has given up the world. He is a sincere man, he wants to do what he preaches." What I mean to say is this, that it represents a tremendous power. What we can do is just to transform it, give it another form. This tremendous power in the hands of the roving Sannyasins of India has got to be transformed, and it will raise the masses up.

Now, you see, we have brought the plan down nicely on paper; but I have taken it, at the same time, from the regions of idealism. So far the plan was loose and idealistic. As years went on, it became more and more condensed and accurate; I began to see by actual working its defects, and all that.

What did I discover in its working on the material plane? First, there must be centres to educate these monks in the method of education. For instance, I send one of my men, and he goes about with a camera: he has to be taught in those things himself. In India, you will find every man is quite illiterate, and that teaching requires tremendous centres. And what does all that mean? Money. From the idealistic plane you come to everyday work. Well, I have worked hard, four years in your country, and two in England. And I am very thankful that some friends came to the rescue. One who is here today with you is amongst them. There are American friends and English friends who went over with me to India, and there has been a very rude beginning. Some English people came and joined the orders. One poor man worked hard and died in India. There are an Englishman and an Englishwoman who have retired; they have some means of their own, and they have started a centre in the Himalayas, educating the children. I have given them one of the papers I have started – a copy you will find there on the table – The Awakened India. And there they are instructing and working among the people. I have another centre in Calcutta. Of course, all great movements must proceed from the capital. For what is a capital? It is the heart of a nation. All the blood comes into the heart and thence it is distributed; so all the wealth, all the ideas, all the education, all spirituality will converge towards the capital and spread from it.

I am glad to tell you I have made a rude beginning. But the same work I want to do, on parallel lines, for women. And my principle is: each one helps himself. My help is from a distance. There are Indian women,

English women, and I hope American women will come to take up the task. As soon as they have begun, I wash my hands of it. No man shall dictate to a woman; nor a woman to a man. Each one is independent. What bondage there may be is only that of love. Women will work out their own destinies – much better, too, than men can ever do for them. All the mischief to women has come because men undertook to shape the destiny of women. And I do not want to start with any initial mistake. One little mistake made then will go on multiplying; and if you succeed, in the long run that mistake will have assumed gigantic proportions and become hard to correct. So, if I made this mistake of employing men to work out this women's part of the work, why, women will never get rid of that – it will have become a custom. But I have got an opportunity. I told you of the lady who was my Master's wife. We have all great respect for her. She never dictates to us. So it is quite safe.

That part has to be accomplished.

❑